GRANDSON
CONVERSATIONS

Ron Klein

Copyright © 2024 Ron Klein
All rights reserved
First Edition

NEWMAN SPRINGS PUBLISHING
320 Broad Street
Red Bank, NJ 07701

First originally published by Newman Springs Publishing 2024

ISBN 979-8-89308-361-3 (Paperback)
ISBN 979-8-89308-362-0 (Digital)

Printed in the United States of America

To the young men who seek understanding
of the world and of themselves.

CONTENTS

Preface vii
Introduction ix

1. Achievements 1
2. Adversity 3
3. Alignment 5
4. Apologies 7
5. Arrogance 9
6. Awkward Conversations 11
7. Bad Bosses 13
8. Beliefs 15
9. Career Success 17
10. Communicating 19
11. Compliments 21
12. Compromises 23
13. Confidants 25
14. Confidences 27
15. Decisions 29
16. Destiny 31
17. Disagreements 33
18. Emotional Displays 35
19. Fairness 37
20. Fathers 39
21. Finances 41
22. I Came Out That Way 43
23. Imago 45

24. Job Security 47
25. Keep a Journal 49
26. Listening 51
27. Luck 53
28. Marrying 55
29. Mentors and Sages 57
30. Near-Term Goals 59
31. Perseverance 61
32. Personality Types 63
33. Problems 65
34. Reading 67
35. Reliability 69
36. Sages 71
37. Semantics 73
38. Stories 75
39. Stress 77
40. The Future 79
41. The Halo Effect 81
42. The Ideal Day 83
43. The Next Decade 85
44. The Path Not Taken 87
45. The Thinking of Others 89
46. Time Management 91
47. Tribes 93
48. Victimization 95
49. Wealthy People 97
50. Women 99

PREFACE

Initially, I wrote these one-page essays as a means to connect with my grandson who lives across the country. We don't often see each other, and when we do, it's rarely one-on-one time. He doesn't know what aspects of life to ask about, and I'm averse to preaching to him on the rare occasion when I see him.

INTRODUCTION

This is not a book that one should sit down and read on a Sunday afternoon. My recommendation is to read one essay a day. This method will facilitate contemplation.

It's difficult to imagine that each essay will engage the reader. Some may seem simple. "Everyone knows that." Other may elicit some insight, introspection, and changed behaviors. It's possible that, for a handful, the reader will underline sentences, use marginalia asterisks and notes, and then be tabbed for future reference. As the author, I, too, have my favorites and some that don't seem as useful. My hope is that before you get to day 50, you've concluded that the book was worth more than you paid for it.

ESSAY 1

Achievements

When we graduate from high school, we celebrate. Rightfully so. We've completed a long endeavor. Later, when we achieve certifications, a college degree, or a license, we pause and take pride in having attained a goal we've pursued. When I received my baccalaureate degree, I stood a little taller. I raised a toast to myself when I got my private pilot's license and then, again, when I got my commercial pilot's license and again with each additional aircraft category rating I received. We celebrate when we get our first professional position in our field and, again, when we get promoted.

These achievements are important. In our professional lives, they're indications that we're progressing. In our personal lives, achievements strengthen us because, each time, we set a goal, diligently pursued it, and then reached it. Some personal examples are running a marathon or getting a scuba diving certification. These achievements add to our self-confidence and set the mindset habit of pursuing improvement.

But sometimes, we can get so focused on a goal that we lose perspective. We see it as the mountaintop destination rather than an incremental step. An Olympic gold medalist told me that a few days after receiving her gold medal, she entered a phase of depression. What's next? She had worked so diligently and exclusively on this singular goal for so long that she lost sight of the fact that she had a life to live. We see this same effect on men who have created a successful business, written a best-selling book, were promoted to general officer, or achieved the lifelong goal of being the lead architect designing a new hospital. After the toasts, the inevitable question comes: What's next?

Over the course of your life, you'll go through several transition points. These may include your first professional position, marriage, having children, important career successes, buying a home, becoming an empty nester, and retirement. There's a reason that school graduations are called *commencements* rather than *achievements*. We celebrate the accomplishment, but we want the graduating students to turn their attention to tomorrow when he/she *commences* with the next phase of life's journey. A mountaintop achievement is the culmination of this particular goal. Don't confuse it with a satisfying life.

ESSAY 2

Adversity

You're going to go through hard times. Perhaps you are right now. Typically, young people struggle more with adversity. Perhaps it's the shock of it. There's also affront at the unfairness of it. In the decades ahead, you won't be as surprised when it comes. It's never welcome, but if we're healthy, there comes a point when we say to ourselves, "Here we go again."

Talk with someone older. Ask them about the canyons of their life. In nearly every instance, they will tell you these were the periods of their greatest growth. The difficult times bring discouragement, impoverishment, emotional pain, a wound to self-worth, and/or a sense of no path forward. But when you get to the other side, you'll understand the phrase "The north wind created the Vikings."

Consider men who appear to be the epitome of success. They have career success, the respect of their peers, friends, a devoted wife, and the esteem of their community. I know several of these men, and each one overcame adversity that could have been debilitating. There may be men who excelled in an Ivy League university, then, through their connections, got a great job, and then, with the right bosses, had a smooth path to professional and personal successes. But I've never met one.

The tough times make you appreciative. If you've had times in your life when you put $10 worth of gas in your car to get you to payday, then you'll appreciate filling your gas tank each time you stop at the gas station. When you work a second job to save money for the down payment on a house, you'll be grateful for a hard-earned home. I have a friend who takes weeklong trips canoeing the Boundary Waters. He does this for the experience and the beauty but also because it increases his appreciation for his everyday life when he sleeps in a warm bed.

Adversity also brings compassion. You'll talk with someone who's struggling with a job loss, and you'll remember being dismissed because a nephew of the business owner needed a job.

If you're insightful, the hard times will increase your understanding of how the world works. You'll immediately recognize the difference between someone who attributes their circumstance to bad luck and someone with grit.

When you encounter and prevail through the difficult times, you'll learn that you're tougher than you knew. Each round strengthens you and increases your resilience.

ESSAY 3

Alignment

Adults of all ages get frustrated because their lives are not the way they'd like them to be. A primary reason for this is unrealistic expectations. Another reason is that we're not intentional with our time, energy, and attention. We frequently fail to align our limited time with what's important to us.

A common error is to underestimate the time it takes to maintain. Whether it's a relationship or a skill, we somehow think once it's established, it won't require ongoing effort. The second law of thermodynamics states that, left unattended, order becomes disorder. We see this all around us. As you walk through a century-old abandoned manufacturing building, the rusting pipes and corroded machinery are evident. Anyone who has had a physical injury and had been unable to exercise for months will tell you about his/her fitness decline. Without constant attention, the garden becomes overgrown.

This physical law has an analogy to our skills and relationships. If you've learned a foreign language and haven't used it in years, your fluency declines. When I was a young man, my best friend and I explored the state on our motorcycles. Then I moved out of state, and our relationship faded. We didn't nurture our friendship, and now, when we run into each other, our conversations lack depth.

Marriages deteriorate when you don't have date nights. If your work is all-consuming, you won't be a present, available, and guiding father. My children are grown and have their own families. Consequently, I have far less time with them. Friendships are important to me. Seven times last month, I met a friend for breakfast or lunch. In addition, I spent four evenings in men's groups. I've identified what's important to me and invest accordingly.

You need to identify what contributes to the quality of your life. This will change. Your priorities should be different when you're twenty-five and single than when you're thirty-five and have young children. Once you've identified what's most valuable, it's essential that you then dedicate the requisite time and attention. The greatest challenge here is deciding what you're *not* going to do. Write down what's most important to you and then apply a reasonable estimate of how many hours a month you need to give each of these priorities. Next, decide what you need to quit doing or, perhaps, spend less time doing. Being overcommitted is a choice. So is allocating your time to matters of lesser value.

ESSAY 4

Apologies

Few men are adept at expressing frustration and hurt. Even fewer know how to apologize. And still fewer understand the consequences of accepting apologies. Reputations, and even friendships, are lost because of missing or ineffective apologies. Many of us are confounded to see estranged sibling and parent relationships when it appears that a simple apology would restore families. Skilled customer service people at retailers like Nordstrom know how to apologize. Irate customers express their aggravation and, in the end, are satisfied and leave as an even more loyal Nordstrom customer than they were before the incident. If you know people who are adept at apologies, you may use adjectives like *gracious*.

Let's begin with how to express a frustration or hurt emotions. Avoid accusatory language. Don't say to your wife, "Why do you always criticize me when I stop off with the guys for a beer after work?" Rather, say something like, "Can we come up with an agreeable arrangement for me to spend time with my friends?" The first statement is a personal attack. The second statement is an invitation for a conversation. Secondly, keep your priorities in mind. Do you want to complain about how she leaves the cap off the toothpaste, keeps hitting the snooze button on her alarm, or has a cluttered closet? Or do you want to look at this woman who does so much for you, who loves you deeply, and decide not to comment on inconsequential annoyances? Remind yourself that you have some practices she accepts.

Also, don't let repeated irritations build until they erupt with much more anger than is warranted. If the annoyance is going to subside in a few minutes, let it go. If this is the third time and each time you're getting more resentful, calm down and then voice the matter before it festers any longer.

You're going to be apologizing a lot in your lifetime. This is because sometimes, we're thoughtless, and sometimes we're jerks. When someone tells us we've wronged them, avoid becoming defensive. If you owe an apology, calmly tell the person you erred. Be specific and empathize with how your statement (or action) offended them. Don't explain. Don't justify. Any response that contains the word *but* cancels the apology. On the contrary, it aggravates the situation.

Accepting someone's apology is a more difficult decision than most people realize. If you accept the other person's apology, the matter is closed. It's over with. It's done. You can't bring it up again. If you're still riled, you may want to take a walk around the block before you accept someone's apology.

Finally, there will be times where you don't feel like you owe the other person an apology. In these situations, you'll need to ask yourself whether it's better to clear the air and set the record straight or whether it's more important to preserve the relationship. This answer will be different for a difficult coworker than it will be for a long-standing friend.

ESSAY 5

Arrogance

Coming to accurately know one's self is a lifelong pursuit. For the vast majority of us, our default setting is to consider that we're better than we are. You may have seen the statistic that 80 percent of drivers think they are safer than the average driver. The fact is, we *want* to believe we're more honest, kinder, and smarter than others. This self-deceit impedes our character development.

We all know people who don't just think they're above average but truly believe they're superior to the rest of us. Such narcissism has always baffled me. In every field, there are people who are better than you. More to the point, even if you truly are in the top 1 percent of your field, you should be humbled by what you don't know and can't do. Can you make a steady chair? Can you console a couple who lost their child? Can you sew a pair of pants that fit? Can you create performance metrics for an organization? Can you compare one balance sheet to the next one and detect adverse trends? Can you accurately diagnose an ill child? To think that what you do well is the most important of human contributions is arrogance stacked upon arrogance.

Though less common, we can also err because we don't recognize our abilities. Because we write well, we think it's ordinary. If math is intuitive and enjoyable, we may not see ourselves as exceptional. If you're a concrete sequential thinker, you may not recognize the advantage this brings to complex problems. If you're naturally relational, you may not appreciate the benefit you have in first impressions. I have a friend who is an exceptional interviewer but thinks this is an ordinary skill. Most people are familiar with Lao Tzu's admonition to never underestimate your enemy. But you can also err by underestimating your capabilities.

Your goal should be to have a realistic understanding of your relative knowledge and skills. Acknowledgments and awards provide insight. The most accurate of these are peer recognitions. The compliments you receive provide clues. Perhaps you've heard comments like the following: "You're an incisive thinker. You look at complex matters and then identify the crux of the matter." This likely reveals a skill that you may not recognize.

It's difficult to overstate the importance of pursuing an accurate assessment of yourself. Several times, I've seen men self-destruct because they became overconfident in their abilities. They focused on their strengths and downplayed their shortcomings. They were attentive to their position rather than the corresponding responsibilities. They were deluded by the attention leaders receive. This is another instance where mentors, and especially confidants, are helpful. You need to have some men in your life who know you and will tell you the truth. Regularly ask them what they see.

ESSAY 6

Awkward Conversations

When I was a young man, I bought a new red sports car. It cost more than was prudent, but I had a young man's priorities. I loved that car. It rarely had dirt on it. One day, a classmate asked me if we could trade cars for a few days. During spring break, he planned to visit family on the Navaho reservation, and the reliability of his car was questionable. His request completely caught me off guard. I hemmed and hawed. I don't remember what I said, but it was probably something along the line of, "Let me think about it." Eventually, I made some excuse and said I couldn't. I lied. What I should have said was, "No! I've driven on those washboard dirt roads, and it's nuts to think I'd let you take my car." But I wanted to be nice. I confused *direct* with *rude*.

You've undoubtedly encountered similar conversations and will again and again. Perhaps you're single, and a friend says she'd like to set you up for a date with someone whom you casually know. Your immediate thought is, *No! I don't find her attractive, and her manner is brusque.* But what you say is, "Give me a few days to consider this." I've never found a muddled equivocal response to be helpful. Doing so creates unnecessary personal anguish, and it gives the other person hope where there is none. A better response is, "I'm sure she's a nice person, but she isn't my type."

You want to be polite and respectful while also being direct. A few days ago, an acquaintance gave me a persuasive presentation on his new business and asked me to invest. I like him and expect to see him at a monthly men's group. But he has a terrible track record of start-up investments. I said, "Thanks for thinking of me, but the amount of funds I've allocated for speculative investments is at my limit."

Sometimes you'll be willing to try a smaller bite than is being offered. As an example, a man you barely know says, "A few of us are taking a three-day deep-sea fishing trip. Would you like to join us?" Your response may be, "I don't know you very well. After your trip, I'd like to meet you for lunch or drinks after work." This is a truthful and respectful response. A friend of mine who is a financial planner recently did this. A wealthy man whom he'd like as a client invited him to go on a four-day casino gambling trip. My friend said, "I can't get away for that long, but if you ever take a one-day trip, I'd like to join you." The wealthy man was delighted. He planned a one-day trip, my friend went, and the man became a client.

An acquaintance will avoid offense and tell you something nice. A friend will be kind and tell you what you need to hear. Learn to be kind.

ESSAY 7

Bad Bosses

The vast majority of us get to experience a bad boss. This is because they outnumber the good ones. Sometimes we regret not having been more careful in accepting the position. Sometimes our supervisor takes another position, and his/her replacement is the bad boss. Regardless of how this came about, we experience a precipitous decline in the quality of our work life.

I put bad bosses into one of two categories: the inept and the unethical. Inept supervisors are disorganized, micromanage, provide little or no feedback, show favoritism, take credit for another's work, constantly change priorities, and/or criticizes without providing guidance. This is just the beginning. There's a long list of bad-boss characteristics. (It's important to note that a demanding boss, one with high expectations, can be a very good boss.)

You can learn a lot from bad bosses. To cite just one example, I was a soldier assigned to an Army armor (tank) company. We were instructed to have completed breakfast and be prepared to take the tanks to the firing range at 7:00 a.m. Around 7:20 a.m., we were informed that there was a delay. No one told us what the cause was or when we might proceed. After two frustrating idle hours, we proceeded. I swore that if I ever became a supervisor, I'd keep my subordinates informed. I kept that vow.

When you get a bad boss, don't respond by slacking off. Be true to who you are. Don't go to his/her supervisor to inform on your boss. This will indicate disloyalty on your part. They won't want you on their team in the future. Besides, they already know.

In well-run organizations, bad bosses have short tenures. Senior managers become aware, and they know the damage taking place. Examples are losing good employees and alienating clients. In poorly run organizations, bad bosses can remain in place for years. If after a few months, there doesn't seem to be any movement, it's often best to look for another position, either elsewhere in the organization or with another employer. On occasion, a senior manager is aware and will take you aside and tell you how valuable you are. If this happens, politely ask when you might be given another opportunity within the organization. This alerts them that they have a short time frame to resolve the matter. If they provide an equivocal reply, this lets you know that change is not imminent. Now you're left with: accept it or leave it.

If you get an unethical boss, this is a serious matter. If you do nothing, your reputation is endangered. You can even risk legal liability. On the other hand, it's risky, and it takes deftness to elevate this to senior management. In these situations, you need to seek the counsel of your mentor.

ESSAY 8

Beliefs

People have all sorts of beliefs. Middle-age men with a pot gut think young women find them attractive. People believe in ghosts. Some people are polytheists, others are monotheists, and others are atheists. People believe all wealthy people are greedy. Addicts don't believe they are addicted. Despite evidence to the contrary, people believe themselves to be good neighbors and citizens. People believe government is the solution, and people believe the government is the problem. People believe their pets will be with them in heaven. People believe what they do for a living is a greater contribution to society than what others do. As a general statement, people prefer to believe that which they prefer to be true.

Oftentimes, we get frustrated with people for their beliefs. This may be because their beliefs contradict ours, or it may be that their beliefs impede relationships or workplace collaboration. Sometimes we just get frustrated with stupidity. A common error is to use reason to alter someone's beliefs. Don't. This only serves to frustrate both you and the other person. Many beliefs are emotionally based. Just as it's ineffective to use emotions to counter facts, it's equally futile to use facts in response to emotions.

You may know people who want their beliefs challenged. I belong to two groups of men who meet monthly for the express purpose of discussing ideas to increase their knowledge and changing their positions on issues. These people are the minority. When you identify them, mentally put them in a different category.

In the workplace, there are times when someone's opinion needs to be changed. A business example is that there are only enough resources to pursue expanded marketing plans or to upgrade the facility. Enterprises that have measurable outcomes (e.g., manufacturing, business, and engineering) will have a decision-making process and someone with clear authority to make the final decision. Nonprofits, universities, churches, and other organizations that don't have outcome metrics will typically have lengthy collaboration practices that value cordiality over efficiency or effectiveness.

Finally, semantics are important. An unfortunate development has been the emergence of statements like *your* truth and *my* truth. Truth is fact-based. Six times seven equals forty-two, or it doesn't. It's 684 air miles from here to the Nashville airport, or it isn't. It's important to recognize the distinction between opinions and facts. You may be cold, and I may be hot, but we shouldn't be in disagreement as to whether the temperature is 72°F.

ESSAY 9

Career Success

It's not uncommon for young men to have high career aspirations. They ask, "How do I reach the top of my career field?" The more profound question is, *should* this be your preeminent goal? There are significant trade-offs when you pursue an all-consuming goal. These include the relationship ones of being a good husband, father, and friend. They also include the personal ones of hobbies, travel, and other interests. I know of no one who is at the top of his/her career field and has a well-rounded life. These are incompatible goals. A life well lived is the topic for another day. I'll constrain this essay to men in their twenties who aspire (and perhaps should) to achieve the top rung of the ladder.

Begin by being attentive to the path and practices of those who have succeeded. What positions did they hold when they were young men? How long did they stay in one position before moving to another? What technical qualifications do they have? How did they come to the attention of senior leaders who later placed them in key positions? While this is a recommended practice, emulating successful people entails three important challenges.

One difficulty is success comes from tenaciously doing ordinary things well. Magazine articles, blogs, and guest speakers don't address this. Audiences want to hear about the exciting, bold moves. But to get helpful insight, you need to look at how the successful person spent the preponderance of his/her time.

A second difficulty associated with emulating the success of others is that you don't have the same personalities. Look at the leaders in your field and consider how much they have in common. In business, there's wide variation. One sees successful leaders who seek attention and some who are practically recluses. Some are relational, and others are analytical. Some are methodical, and others are innovative. Conversely, in the military, senior officers have similar attributes. You can, and should, adapt to what is required to be successful. At the same time, be realistic about whether your core personality is compatible with the attributes of senior leaders in your field.

Third, the world changes. Technology changes. Consumer tastes change. Competitors change. Societal values change. Strictly following the career path of current leaders is unlikely to succeed.

An aspect of success that's seldom studied is why things went wrong. In last year's Indianapolis 500 race, thirty-three cars started, but only seventeen finished. Far too often, people are so focused on winning that they forget about not failing. Scrutinize failures. Who was a rising star with great promise who derailed? Did he get full of himself and lose focus on his responsibilities? Was it sexual misconduct? Did he become dismissive of subordinates? Did he think technical expertise alone was sufficient? Did his peers quit supporting him because he wasn't a team player? Be one of the few people who are especially attentive to career failures.

ESSAY 10

Communicating

The reason we go to a venue to hear a speaker is because oratory is so effective. I attended an event when Colin Powell spoke and another when Condoleezza Rice was the presenter. In both instances, there were no graphics or summarizing points on an accompanying screen. The power was from the speaker alone. When we have a one-on-one conversation, we pick up on skepticism when we notice the other person's eyebrows arch. We have the tone of their words. As we exchange thoughts, the conversation takes us in unexpected directions. Estimates are 70 percent to 90 percent of communication is nonverbal. As an example, consider storytelling, the most memorable and impactful means by which we learn and remember. Face-to-face is the richest communication means.

In many cases, the written word is the optimal communication means (consider this document). Writing requires that you organize your thoughts. Writing gives you the opportunity to take time to analyze and describe the points you want to make. A written document provides the recipient the opportunity to read it (and reread it) at his/her time of choosing. The recipient will underline key points and use marginalia to prepare responses or cite similar instances. A document has the advantage of clarity. People don't come back later and say, "I thought you said…" Another advantage of writing is that we read twice as fast as someone speaks. Finally, a document has permanence. Much later, we're able to reference the written word.

Telephone calls are not as rich as face-to-face, but this form of communication is much more efficient. There's the opportunity for back-and-forth responses to what's been said. By listening to tone and pauses, you can pick up on the other person's enthusiasm or hesitancy. Video calls have the added advantage of facial expressions.

Texting and emails have the advantage of immediacy. "I'm running ten minutes late for our lunch meeting." Electronic communications are suited to short single-topic questions and notifications. At the same time, because electronic communications are so abbreviated, they lack verbal and facial cues and don't convey emotions. They often result in miscommunication of intent.

Nearly everyone has a preferred means of communication. I know people who pick up the phone in an instant. I know others who have an aversion to phone calls. I have a friend who has a strong preference for face-to-face. It's difficult to get him to respond to an email or text message. In order to succeed in relationships, personal and professional, you need to use the communication means best suited for the situation. Does the communication include emotions? Is there a need for a back-and-forth exchange of ideas? Success requires that you're skilled in each form of communication and attentive to use the one that's appropriate for the situation.

ESSAY 11

Compliments

Everyone appreciates a sincere compliment. The effort it takes to provide acknowledgment to someone is far outweighed by the value. Several years ago, I was at the home of a friend who was hosting a backyard dinner for several Vietnamese business owners. I knew the business owners because I had gone to Vietnam to teach best business practices and provide consulting. At the dinner buffet line, there was a stack of large red plastic cups and a marker. The Vietnamese business owner in front of me was unaware of the American custom of writing your name on your cup so that throughout the evening, you knew your cup from the others. When I noticed the puzzled look on his face, I picked up the black marker and wrote on his cup: "Mr. Quan: The quiet intellectual one." Three years later, at another event, Mr. Quan's wife told me, "He still has that cup."

Establish a habit of complimenting people. This may be a cheerful person at the counter of a busy coffee shop. It may be the grocery worker who is attractively arranging the produce. It may be a conference presenter who clearly communicated a topic of value.

When you regularly interact with someone, be alert to what he/she pays special attention to. It may be his knowledge of wine pairings, her artistic earrings, his unflappable demeanor under stress, or her consistently thorough preparation. In these situations, make a point to compliment the person on whatever it is that they take special pride in doing.

Most people are quick to differentiate flattery from sincere compliments. The reason for your comment should be simple kindness, not because you expect that you'll accrue *points* with the person, or he/she will be more inclined to accede to your requests.

ESSAY 12

Compromises

When I owned a company, I determined and then communicated to employees our nonnegotiable core values. I repeatedly said, "We'll make mistakes, but if you violate one of these rules, you're done." As an example, one of these core values was telling the truth. I said if you lie to a client, one another, or to me, that'll be your last day. Then of course, I had to follow through when someone was dishonest.

The company had expertise in an area that would benefit a client. We had just received a small contract, and I was hopeful that this client would result in substantial growth. Then I received a call from the company owner. He was the sort of person who accrues loyalty to himself by arranging favors. He told me he was ready to award us some work, but he needed something from me. He wanted me to employ two men. He went further and set their salaries. I told him I couldn't do that. These salaries would be in excess of what current employees with greater expertise had, and I was committed to compensation aligned with contributions. We didn't get the contract, and the company didn't experience the growth I had projected. The moment I was on the phone with him, I knew what I'd be compromising. I've never regretted my response. I knew what that compromise would entail.

Compromises are daily decisions, one of the lubricants of life. The vast majority of them are minor and necessary. Sometimes we compromise too often and get taken advantage of. When we compromise infrequently, we're the selfish one. It's the compromises of your values, of who you are, that require you to stop and focus. Sometimes the compromise decision is abrupt (like this example). Other times, the compromises are minor and gradual. One day you come to the realization that you're becoming someone you don't want to be, and/or your reputation is in jeopardy. Now it's decision time.

When possible, decide in advance what's nonnegotiable. Are you willing to misrepresent something, perhaps dishonesty by omission? What is stretching a bit about your capabilities, and at what point are you claiming expertise that you don't have? Perhaps your boss says, "Oh, this is a common industry practice. Everyone does it." Some compromises will alter who you are.

ESSAY 13

Confidants

Confidants are essential. Casual friends come easily. Close friends require a regular investment of time. But confidants require trust, time, vulnerability, and an emotional investment. The number of confidants a man has is always going to be small. I know of no one who has more than three. But disturbingly, the most common number is 0. This is tragic for two reasons: we need others, and others need us.

One reason for confidants is we regularly encounter ordinary frustrations. These range from a difficult boss to misbehaving children to insufficient hours in the week to meet obligations. Women frequently want affirmation from their confidants. They want reassurance that they're good mothers or are justified by irritations over sexist remarks at work. Typically, when men vent frustrations, they aren't seeking reassurance. A simple acknowledgment suffices; e.g., "That sucks, man."

A second and very important reason to have confidants is our need for perspective. None of us have an accurate image of ourselves. We justify and excuse and blame. A confidant calls us out when we look everywhere except in the mirror. He asks what role we had in the circumstance. He asks questions to help us explore our options. He helps us separate wishful thinking from what's realistic. This is how we become better, not only with a particular issue but as men.

Third, the day is coming when you're going to encounter a deep hole. It may be a job loss, your wife's cancer, personal finances, or something else. When men encounter the really tough times alone, bad things happen. Examples include marital infidelity, addictions, and depression. Men need confidants so that when these times come, as they inevitably will, we have and are able to provide support.

Some men who have no male confidants will say their wife fills this role. This position has several difficulties. One is that your wife is the sole recipient of your complaints. You need her affection, but then you burden her with the incompatible responsibility to tell you hard truths. Also, sometimes you need clarity on issues you have with her. She wants a different vacation than you do. She feels like you're neglecting her and your children if you go out with the guys one night a month. Are you being selfish by not wanting to spend another weekend at her parents' home?

Finally, if your wife is your sole confidant, you need to ask yourself why. Is it because you hold the view that a *real* man doesn't need anyone? Is it because you're unwilling to invest the time and emotional energy to develop a confidant relationship?

If you don't have a confidant, go to work on developing one. This is a bit akin to dating. Invite someone you like to go out for lunch. See how the conversation unfolds. Take the lead by talking about something personal. You're likely to have lunches with several men before you identify someone who will become a confidant. This is important. Do it.

ESSAY 14

Confidences

From the time that we're children, our friends tell us secrets, and we promise to keep them. When we get into the workforce, we need to appreciate the gravity of confidences. In your twenties, your supervisor may ask you about whether a coworker is working the hours that he/she is reporting. In your thirties, you may participate in discussions regarding which candidate to hire. In your forties, you may be privy to employee salaries. Later, you might be in board meetings of a nonprofit or civic organization deciding who should be asked to fill key positions. One of the crucial characteristics of a professional is the ability to keep these confidences.

I belong to a civic organization of professionals who work to improve our community. At one of the committee meetings, there was a discussion about selecting someone for a board position. The committee decided against a nominee under consideration because he was considered unreliable. One of the committee members relayed this to the nominee. The leadership was able to identify who had violated the vow of confidence. Her membership in the organization was terminated and her professional reputation seriously damaged.

I've seen promising young men not get selected for leadership positions. They have excellent technical skills and management potential, but they aren't considered to be sufficiently discreet. Managers have heard them relay disparaging rumors about someone.

You may encounter instances of fraud, sexual harassment, or other potential crimes when it's necessary to apprise the leadership. When possible, do this without identifying the source. Effective leaders, once they know what to look for, will pursue the matter.

A few years ago, I was on a corporate board of directors. The company chief financial officer called me. He was clearly nervous and asked me for complete confidentiality, and I agreed. When we met, he brought documents to show me that the chief executive officer was misappropriating funds. He didn't want to be identified as the one who revealed this. He needed the job and was concerned about being fired. Secondly, he understood that his personal reputation would be jeopardized. If it came to be known that he was the source of this information, few other companies would consider him for a position. I assured him that this disclosure would not be traced back to him. I asked him to keep the documents. That afternoon, I called another board member who had responsibility to oversee financial matters. A few days later, he requested an audit of the CEO's expenditures. He then provided the audit results to the board president. The outcome was the dismissal of the chief executive officer. The board identified and documented the problem sooner than they would have otherwise, and no one ever suspected the chief financial officer was the source.

Except for extreme situations, disclosing a confidence is an error from which you'll never recover. Although this essay addresses the professional consequences, it's important to note that breaking confidences will also do irreparable harm to personal relationships.

ESSAY 15

Decisions

Every hour, we make decisions. Most of these are so minor that we don't even recognize them. We establish habits to relieve ourselves of the mental workload associated with routine decisions. When making decisions, I ask myself two questions: Is the decision reversible? What are the consequences of the decision?

The decision to get a tattoo is practically irreversible. When you're twenty-five years old, you might be enamored with the phrase *carpe diem* and get this as a tattoo to show the world how carefree and spontaneous you are. When you're fifty-five years old, this may not be a preeminent value reflecting who you are. If you buy a new car and decide you don't like it, that's a fairly expensive decision to reverse. Conversely, if you buy a used car and don't like it, you can alter this decision within a week or two at a relatively low cost. I have a brother who got a finance degree and later decided to become an educator. That decision was reversible but expensive; i.e., two more years of college. The research and mental energy you put into a decision should be commensurate with how reversible it is.

A second (and independent) consideration is the consequences of a decision that turns out to be the wrong one. If you choose a restaurant for lunch, and the food or service is poor, this is a temporary annoyance. If you accept a job in another city that turns out to be miserable, this will be consequential. Conversely, if you decline to move to another city for a great career opportunity because you're comfortable where you are, although less obvious, this, too, may be a consequential mistake. When considering decisions, one of the questions I ask myself is: Will this be important in five years? It's probable that the most consequential decision you'll ever make is who to marry.

Avoid excessive decision regret. We all get decisions wrong. For some reason, we remember wrong decisions with much greater intensity than the right ones. I've forgotten about a good decision I made last week, but decades later, I remember an answer I got wrong on a driver's training test.

All important decisions entail unknowns. Some of these unknowns could have been discovered if we'd done more research and asked the right questions. When you reflect on these decision errors, make a note so that you'll get better at decision-making. But be careful to note that one can't go through life investigating every aspect of every decision. That'd be overwhelming. Secondly, some of the unknowns are unknowable. Many of our decisions are like the game of poker. You don't know what cards the other player has or what cards are in the deck. You can play a perfect hand and still lose.

Mistakes are inevitable. Don't hold on to regrets about decision mistakes of five or ten years ago.

ESSAY 16

Destiny

Around the seventh or eighth grade, school administrators ask parents to prompt their children to advocate for themselves. In high school, students should have the fortitude and communication skills to ask teachers what they need to do in order to improve their grades. When parents protect their older teenagers from resolving difficulties, they handicap them. Beginning with our early teenage years, we need to make and take responsibility for our decisions.

Perhaps you're one of the 1 percent of children who were raised by two knowledgeable, engaged, thoughtful, and encouraging parents who guided you to good decisions and inspired the best in you. This topic is for the rest of us. The vast majority of us were raised in a home where our parents were never in contention for the parents of the year award. There are myriad reasons for this. Our parents learned from their parents. They have their own insecurities, odd ideas, other priorities, and sometimes mental health issues. One has to take a driver's test to demonstrate a basic level of proficiency before you're allowed on the road, but there's no competency test required to become a parent.

By osmosis, you unknowingly absorb the ideas and practices of your household. Your speech patterns, humor, guilt, ability to forgive slights, view of the world, and your own potential are but a few of attributes and attitudes that accompany you into adulthood.

But while the parenting we received has great influence, you need to avoid accepting your upbringing as the template for your life. Beginning in childhood, we visit the homes of our friends. We notice the differences in their households compared to ours. This accelerates as we enter our early twenties. We're increasingly exposed to a wide variety of people and the choices they make. The attitudes and perspective that you inherited only becomes your destiny if you choose it to be so. By the time you're twenty-five years old, you have enough exposure to the world and enough maturity to be responsible for the choices you make and who you are. You no longer have the excuse of blaming your upbringing.

Consider the alternative. I've heard thirty-year-olds say, "My father had a quick temper, and I do too." I've heard thirty-five-year-olds explain their debt by saying, "Yeah, my parents always spent every dime they had, and I never learned to be thrifty." Statements like this come from men who decided not to take control of their life. "I am who I am. That's the way I was raised." What a terrible abdication of control over your life!

Look at the choices others make. Look at their lives. As you pursue self-knowledge and set your path, seek the input of mentors and confidants. In the end, you alone are responsible for the person you become. *I am the captain of my ship.*

ESSAY 17

Disagreements

A valuable skill to learn is how to disagree. The first principle to keep in mind is that you're disagreeing with an idea, not a person. I often think of the format of high school debates. Students begin by stating the topic, followed by a definition of terms. Workplace and personal disagreements won't (and shouldn't) be as formal, but it helps if you keep this recipe in mind. I can't tell you how many times I've been in disagreement, only to learn that our differences are over terms.

The most common mistake is disagreements become a contest. This means one party will eventually win, and the other will lose. Men are especially prone to this error. If you're engaged in this conversation to understand the other person's perspective, a contest mindset hinders you. This is because instead of listening to truly understand, you listen to retort. If you're engaged in this conversation to persuade, putting the other person in the position of defending himself results in resistance on his/her part rather than receptivity.

As soon as you recognize that a win-lose contest is unfolding, stop. Ask the other person to restate their position. Reassure them that you respect them. Tell them which parts of their arguments you agree with. Repeating what they've said gives them the respect that you're listening.

It's imperative that, to the extent possible, you remove emotions from the discussion. "Will this lower-priced service level result in some of our current customers switching?" will elicit a different reaction than "Implementing your recommendation will result in lower profit margins." Avoid using the terms *you* and *your*. These words make the disagreement personal rather than about the idea.

Don't stay in a discussion when the other party isn't interested in listening. I was a board member of an organization and engaged in a one-on-one discussion with the senior executive. He was advocating for a position that I didn't think was tenable. Each time I explained my concerns, he was immediately dismissive and reiterated why his high-risk untested program should be pursued. After the third time he did this, I stood up and said that I was leaving. I said, "You're not listening to me, so there's no point in continuing this discussion." (To his credit, he acknowledged his behavior and asked me to sit down, and then he listened.) When you find yourself in situations where there isn't an exchange of ideas, stop engaging. One technique is silence. Just stop responding. Sometimes this resets the dialogue.

Also, don't let the discussion get diverted. Remind the other person of the topic being addressed. If there's another subject, set it aside until the original one is resolved.

Having constructive disagreements is a difficult skill to learn. When you see someone who does this well, pay close attention to how they respond. Achieving this skill will take you far, both professionally and in your personal life.

ESSAY 18

Emotional Displays

You may encounter bosses who are screamers. Everyone I've known has been male. They're bullies: loud, threatening, mercurial, and intimidating. Because employees fear them, they can get quite a bit done—in the short run. But they're never successful in the long run. First, it's the stellar employees who leave. Their reputation allows them to quickly find a position elsewhere. Within a few days, they're calling recruiters or contacts at other organizations. Over time, there's high turnover as others leave the hostile environment.

At the other end of the spectrum, there are men who seem to be devoid of emotions. You never see them angry or delighted. They aren't social, encouraging, or energetic. You don't know what they're thinking. Since the environment is set by the leader, the result is a vapid workplace. In instances of independent specialists (e.g., coders, radiologists), these colorless bosses can be acceptable supervisors. But these men don't get promoted and don't succeed in other settings. This is because people want a strong leader.

To succeed in work settings, you need to be intentional and measured when displaying emotions. Getting this right is essential before you'll be considered for promotions. You don't need to come to work each day as an enthusiastic cheerleader, but you do need to inspire people to do their best. How you do this will, in large part, depend on your personality. Look at presenters who engage their audiences by changing their tone, inflection, and level of energy.

The difficulty for most of us is the appropriate use of emotions when correcting unacceptable actions. These may be a peer who isn't doing his/her share or a subordinate. Over the years, I've used different emotional displays to convey my displeasure. But each time, they've been calculated. When supervising young men engaged in physical labor, I've raised my voice and used direct (albeit not demeaning) language in the presence of others. In professional environments, a technique I use is to take the person aside, describe in no uncertain terms what the problem is, state what will not occur again, and end with, "Are we clear?" Then I dismiss him/her.

You need to display emotions at work: compassion, high expectations, inspiration, engagement, values, and sometimes anger. But this should be intentional and measured. You can, and should be, stern without being demeaning. If you had an outburst of anger, you made a mistake. Apologize. You can get away with this occasionally but not frequently. Look at the senior leaders when it comes to encouraging employees and holding them to the standards and emulate them. If you have access to them, ask them how they appropriately use emotions in the workplace.

ESSAY 19

Fairness

Most children grow up in an environment where their parents have control over every aspect of life. Parents decide bedtimes, meals, where to vacation, and what house to buy. So it's natural for children to aspire for the day they'll be a *grown-up* and be able to do whatever they want. Teenagers begin to grasp the understanding that adults aren't all-powerful. But when a teenager laments ("*It's not fair!*"), he/she displays naivete. The world isn't fair. It can't be fair.

To begin with, we'd have to be in agreement on what is *fair*. Are school vouchers fair because they provide parents with greater choices for their children's education? Or are vouchers unfair because of the harm to public education when tax funds are diverted? Is it fair that employers place a higher value on a chemistry degree than one in history? Are the federal income tax rates fair?

Secondly, we know and control far less than we'd like to believe. Ivy League university admissions officers think they can identify the applicants most likely to succeed. They can't. It's impossible to make precise distinctions among a group of highly qualified individuals. If the university can accept two thousand incoming freshmen, the admissions officer should select the top ten thousand applications, toss the folders up in the air, and randomly pick up two thousand. (This would have the added benefit of informing those selected that they aren't superior to their peers. There was luck involved.)

Thirdly, randomness is everywhere. Someone bought Bitcoin and gained $50,000 in six months. Do you believe he's that much smarter than everyone else? There's favoritism. There's misfortune. We make the right decision, but circumstances change. Decisions are made with partial information. I accepted a promising position with a company. Within a few months, it came to light that my supervisor was dishonest. We lost the contract for the project I was working on, and I found myself unemployed. This is the world we live in. When such injustices occur, get mad. Complain to your friends! Then get up the next morning and get on with whatever the next step needs to be.

There are zealots who change society. For an inspiring example, read "Letter from Birmingham Jail." But for the other 99.9 percent of us, we err when we keep getting upset that the world isn't fair. In the workplace and in social settings, if you use the phrase "That's not fair," you lose credibility. This is *not* to suggest that you should passively accept every wrong that you encounter. You should identify and fight the winnable battles. This *is* a recommendation to not get stuck wishing the world were different than it is.

ESSAY 20

Fathers

No role in your life will be more consequential than that of being a father. This is embarking into new territory. I've never known a young man who thought he was qualified to be a father. Infants are vulnerable and helpless. Toddlers are playful, inquisitive, and in constant need of attention. This is when we begin to civilize them. When we see them copy our language and reactions, we moderate it and become better. Watching their unique personalities emerge is a special delight. When to encourage them to stay with an interest and when to let them stop is a constant dilemma. The interests and growth of girls is different than that of boys, but they both have an abiding and innate need for a loving ever-present father. When they reach their twenties, you'll transition to an adult-to-adult relationship with them.

Your responsibilities as a provider and protector become preeminent. Sometimes this means you won't be able to pursue high-risk career opportunities or positions that entail extensive travel. Your time with friends, going to concerts, or taking adventure trips will be constrained. But the rewards far outweigh the costs.

Raising children gives you the opportunity to see the world anew, through their inquisitive minds. Being a teacher is one of the most challenging and rewarding endeavors. This is never more so the case as when you're a father.

You need to be present for your children. From watching you, your children will learn all the important aspects of their character. This includes responses to aggravations and bad breaks, perseverance, attitudes toward work, sustaining a good marriage, self-discipline, compassion, and honesty.

You'll never learn the extent of your influence. Decades from now, when your children become parents, their default will be to raise their children the way they were raised. One day you'll influence grandchildren in ways their parents can't.

Embark on this role with great excitement. It'll be joyful, expensive, delightful, frustrating, heartbreaking, and heartwarming. You'll experience love like you never knew existed. Nothing you do with your life will be as important.

ESSAY 21

Finances

In your twenties, personal finances are constrained. Because your industry expertise is limited, so is your salary. Yet you need a place to live and a reliable car. You also want to meet friends for drinks, go to concerts, and to take vacations. In all aspects of our lives, we compare ourselves. You see other young men driving new cars and vacationing in the Caribbean, while your car is older, and you go camping. What you don't see is that his car is leased, and he'll eventually have to face his onerous credit card balance. In your thirties, you're likely buying and furnishing a house, buying cribs, car seats, and Halloween costumes. Because of babysitter expenses, dinners out with friends cost twice as much as five years ago. During these decades, it seems that there's no end to ever-increasing expenses.

The primary financial challenges during these years is that the rewards for spending are visible and immediate, while the eventual benefits of savings are far off and intangible. For many of us, the enjoyment of a new car is greater than seeing a larger number on our 401(k) monthly statement.

Saving and investing are two of the aspects of your life with a great many unknowns. If you save more than is necessary, you'll forgo current experiences. Conversely, if you save too little, you're likely to live decades with constrained finances. But we don't know what the future brings, neither our income, our investment returns, nor unknown major expenses. Given this, which error do you prefer?

Over the past thirty years, the inflation-adjusted return on the S&P 500 stocks has been 7.146 percent. One twenty-five-year-old decides that his near-term wants are such that he opts out of his employer's 401(k) matching program. His peer enrolls and has $200 a month (which is matched by his employer) deducted from his paycheck. From his employer's options, he selects an S&P 500 index fund. From the age thirty-five forward, both men save the same amount. At the age of seventy, the one who invested from twenty-five to thirty-five has $966,025 more than the first. And this is inflation adjusted.

When you turn forty, or your investments reach $100,000, find an investment adviser. One reason for doing this is so that he/she will help with asset allocation and tax counsel. But the reality is, there's excellent software that will do this for you. The real value of a financial planner is to understand your goals and give you objective advice.

People confuse *wealth accumulation* with *financial security*. I know older men with $2 million in assets who are financially secure, and I know men with $20 million who don't have enough. *Financial security* entails managing your wants as well as disciplined investing. The real value of financial security is not what you can buy. Rather it's living a life when money is no longer important.

ESSAY 22

I Came Out That Way

The most commonly asked question of high school seniors is: What are you going to do next year? Some adults ask this out of courtesy. The savvier person asks because your answer provides insight into who you are. Someone who says, "I plan to become a hyperbaric welder," has a personality that is distinctly different from one who responds, "I've been accepted to the Naval Academy and aspire to become a nuclear submariner." Some high school graduates are clear about their career aspirations. It's also common for college students to change their majors. The stated reason is because he didn't like his initial choice or because he learned of another field that was more appealing. But in our twenties, we're rarely insightful enough to ask what these decisions reflect.

I have a friend who loves business. He's owned or been a partial owner in businesses ranging from car washes to manufacturing. He enjoys the challenges. He's energized by the uncertainty and the quest. He recognizes that he's unusual. He shrugs his shoulders and says, "*I came out that way*." He has great admiration for professionals who hone their skills for decades. That's just not who he is.

At one point, I was enamored with being an aviator. I thought I'd like to fly for a living, perhaps become an airline pilot. Then I came to realize that I didn't really want to fly every day for work. What I loved was *learning* to fly. Once I became qualified in one type of aircraft, I wanted to get certified in another. Being an airline pilot would have been a terrible career choice. By nature, I'm not persistently focused on details, and I would not enjoy a life spent in hotel rooms.

What do your career choices say about you? Geneticists are detail-oriented and analytical. City planners have a big-picture orientation and are analytical. Social workers are big picture-oriented and compassionate. Oncologists are detail-oriented and compassionate. Our lives are easier when we know ourselves (this is a lifelong undertaking). Ask an older insightful person what your choices reveal about your personality.

Last week, someone asked me to lunch to ask for my counsel. A few years ago, he had become the operations officer for an organization in disarray. He established best practices and accountability metrics. Now that things are running smoothly, he's restless. I asked him about his career, and he said, although he worked at one company for decades, his role was as a troubleshooter, moving from one division to another. It's entirely consistent that when he's not repairing something, he's restless. *He came out that way.*

Consider what your choices reveal about your personality. Ask older men what they see. We're more effective and more contented when our paid and volunteer work is aligned with our natural preferences. Note that knowing yourself is *not* to be used as an excuse to avoid the hard work of improving. Rather this is to understand what kind of work is a good fit for you.

ESSAY 23

Imago

Knowing ourselves is an enduring challenge of life. What kind of a person am I? Am I adventurous or steadfast or creative? Oftentimes these self-assessments are aspirational rather than realistic. Also, we downplay or forget the times we operated contrary to our preferred self-image.

Beginning in our teenage years, we begin to create a narrative of our life. Over the next decade or so, we explore, alter, and clarify who we are. By our early thirties, we've created a coherent life story: "I've prevailed over adversity." "I'm on a journey to become the best in my field." "I'm determined to be the father I never had." "I aspire to be seen as the consummate professional."

Consider the compliments that bring the greatest pleasure: "Few people are as kind as you." "I wish I were half as smart as you." "You're so creative." "Given your background, coming this far is an extraordinary achievement." "You're reliable and steadfast." "You're so unconventional and interesting." The dearest compliments reveal the image we have of ourselves.

What is your self-image? This is not how you wish others to see you but rather how you see yourself. Perhaps it's the *warrior*, the *comforter*, the *professor*, the *rebel*, the *professional*, the *adventurer*, the *survivor*, or the *teacher*. Dr. Dan McAdams calls these our imago. When we're introspective, we develop a more accurate imago as we age. Also, if we continue to grow, our imago changes. An example is changing from an *explorer* to a *sage*.

When we live lives contrary to our imago, we experience dissonance. Sometimes this occurs because we don't know ourselves well. I wanted to be a popular speaker. It was years before I learned and accepted that, over time, my words have a positive impact, but I don't have the skills or thinking of an entertainer. Another cause of dissonance may be self-deceit. Or it may be because we're reluctant to accept the need to change identities. These are the times we need to turn to our confidants who know us and will speak the truth.

Contentment requires that we know ourselves and our path. Being an *explorer* is no better or worse than being a *healer*. Changing careers, becoming a father, and retiring are examples of life-transition points when our imago and our paths need to change.

ESSAY 24

Job Security

There are very few fields in which job security is not an issue. One-half of 1 percent of the federal government workers are dismissed for poor performance or misconduct. Public school teachers are another example where job security is not a concern. But these employers are outliers. The great majority of us are rightfully concerned with job security. A competitor comes out with a superior product or service, and your company has layoffs. Companies consolidate and close down operations. Companies are acquired, which results in duplicate positions. Companies outsource operations. Technology adaptation alters jobs in an organization. We are, and should be, concerned with job security. Getting laid off from a job is a painful experience. The loss of income is the immediate difficulty. You'll also have to deal with a demoralizing emotional hit.

I've been inside scores of organizations. In every instance, there are select employees who are widely recognized as being head and shoulders above the others. Depending on the organization, this may be due to their technical expertise, their relationships, their dedication to the mission, or some other attributes. A manager with fifteen subordinates is told that he/she needs to identify five employees to be terminated. The first thing he/she does is pull out the list and put an asterisk by the names of the two employees that are crucial.

Immediately, their names are pulled from deliberations. You want to be one of these two.

Look around your organization and identify who these exceptional employees are. If you're new to the organization, you may have to ask a few of your coworkers. A few months into your job, have a private conversation with your boss and ask him/her who the stellar performers are. Once you've identified these stars, emulate them. What are they doing different than the others? Take them to lunch and ask them for suggestions with respect to how you can improve. If they see you following their advice, they'll continue to assist you.

Sometimes you'll learn that you're in the wrong field. Perhaps the successful people are outgoing connectors, and your strength is in analyses and writing. I know driven people who are poor fits for nonprofit organizations. The employee who pushes for accountability and the pursuit of difficult improvements clashes with relational senior leaders who prioritize congeniality. I worked in a hierarchal organization that was averse to disruptive change. I wanted to make hard decisions, identify best practices, and experiment with new initiatives. I did much better when I left that employer and moved to another.

If you're in an organization and type of work that aligns with your skills and temperament, introduce yourself to the stellar performers and interact with them. If you're in a position where the leaders have different personalities than you, don't operate under the illusion that they'll soon come around to see your potential.

ESSAY 25

Keep a Journal

Twenty-five years ago, I began writing a journal. At one point, I paused for nineteen months. But I missed the value and resumed the practice. I don't keep a journal because I expect anyone else to read it. I don't keep one for nostalgic reasons; i.e., to provoke memories like a high school yearbook. Rather I do so to aid my insight. Writing disciplines one's thinking. I don't write about incidental transitory events. I write to encapsulate my thoughts.

As an analogy, consider a near-miss traffic accident. There's hard braking, the screeching of tires, and you come within inches of a collision. When the moment passes, your adrenaline declines, and normal breathing resumes. What then? Five minutes later, do you proceed with your day, having quickly forgotten about the incident? Or do you incorporate the near-miss lesson and alter your driving as much as you would if there had been a collision? If we're to get better, be it driving or relationships or career moves, we want to take time to assess.

Writing requires us to formulate our thoughts. One man says to himself, "Wow, I had a strong reaction to that comment." Another man pursues introspection. In his journal, he describes why he had a strong reaction. It might take him thirty minutes to write a paragraph. Three days later, he might write another entry that describes why his initial assessment wasn't quite right.

Resolve to write succinctly. Avoid tangential matters that aren't important to the topic you're addressing. Precise writing requires precise thinking. If you're confused about your motives or whether you're rationalizing, have a conversation with a friend. Afterward, make the effort to write your thoughts. You'll be pleasantly surprised at how helpful intentional introspection can be.

A second reason to keep a journal is that it helps keep things in perspective. You come to see minor irritants as just that. When you write about kindness shown by others, good fortune, love, and accomplishments, you become more grateful.

Finally, this practice will improve your writing skills. Be attentive to grammar, punctuation, and extraneous words. Like any skill, we get better not by mere repetition but by consistently doing something well.

ESSAY 26

Listening

I have never figured out why so few people are good listeners. People are drawn to good listeners. They like them. A few years ago, my wife and I interviewed financial planners. During an initial meeting, the financial planner provided a polished summary of his expertise and asset-allocation models that took the client's risk tolerance and age into account. He never asked about our experiences, goals, or concerns. At the next interview, another planner sat down with his blank notepad and asked us to tell him about our lives and aspirations. I don't need to tell you which planner got our account.

My observation is, there are three common obstructive behaviors. One is that many people are just talkative. They enjoy conversations when people interrupt and talk over each other. They don't even notice that others aren't talking. Loquacious people are uncomfortable with even a few seconds of silence. A man I knew called me in an effort to persuade me to subscribe to the services he provided. After thirty minutes, I cut him off and said, "Bill, for the past thirty minutes that we've been on this call, you've spoken for twenty-seven. I'm not going to enter into a relationship with someone who thinks he's nine times smarter than I am." Monitor how much you're talking. If there are two of you, you shouldn't be talking more than half the time. If there are five in the group, you shouldn't be talking more than about 20 percent of the time. (If you're rarely talking, that's a different problem.) When you're talking, you're not learning.

A second practice is failing to inquire about the other person. William Churchill's mother, Jennie Jerome, interacted with the leading political leaders of the time. At one point, a journalist asked her about conversations she'd had with William Gladstone and Benjamin Disraeli (both of who were prime ministers). Her response was, "When I left the dining room after sitting next to Gladstone, I thought he was the cleverest man in England. But when I sat next to Disraeli, I felt that I was the cleverest woman." Disraeli steered the conversation toward her. He asked her questions and intently listened.

A third common practice is to get into a debate mode. When the other person is talking, we're only slightly listening. Our brain is engaged in our retort. Then rather than asking deeper questions, we respond with our views. One technique I use in these situations is to take brief notes when the other person is talking. This conveys to the other person that I'm listening, and when it's my turn to respond, I show respect by not overlooking any of the points he/she made.

A recent medical study found that patients prefer women surgeons. The surgical outcomes of men and women are comparable. But patients prefer women because they listen to them. If you want to get ahead in life, learn to become a good listener.

ESSAY 27

Luck

One day, I walked out of my apartment and encountered a neighbor. I could tell she was distraught, and I asked her how things were going. She and her husband were about to buy their first home, and she just learned that they wouldn't qualify for the mortgage because their monthly debt payments were too great. The mortgage originator suggested that if they eliminated a car payment, they'd meet the threshold. The problem was they had two days to show proof that they no longer had this loan. That day, I got a deal on a nice car. I was lucky. So was she.

Another time, I was the one primarily responsible to identify and hire a new senior executive officer for an organization. We interviewed candidates and identified a finalist. In performing our due diligence, we contacted all his references. We identified and spoke to people we knew whom he hadn't provided as references. We had a thorough process, which we followed. Four months after he took the position, I learned that he was misappropriating funds. We didn't have faulty procedures. We were unlucky.

When good fortune comes along, our first inclination is to pat ourselves on the back. There are two primary reasons for this. One is we're predisposed to attribute to ourselves skill, judgment, and expertise. Naturally, I prefer to believe I'm that good. A second impediment is that we like to believe that we have more control over our lives than we do. We don't like to think that our lives are surrounded by too much randomness. The stoic philosopher Seneca said, "Luck is what happens when preparation meets opportunity." This is a pleasant, even inspiring, thought. Furthermore, there's some truth to this quote. But the implication is, we influence what happens. To some degree, we do. But we err when we deny the existence of luck.

On April 10, 2023, a gunman opened fire at a bank in downtown Louisville. A senior police officer, Cory Galloway, and his rookie partner, Nickolas Wilt, were the first on the scene. After Officer Galloway was shot in his vest, he fell down and took cover behind a concrete barrier. He then fired on the gunman and killed him. Afterward, the Louisville Metro Police Department wanted to know whether they were lucky (with the experienced Officer Galloway being the first on the scene) or whether the credit for this outcome could be attributed to the agency's training. This is exactly the right question to ask! A lesser professional would have simply said, "We're that good," and closed the matter. In this case, the investigation attributed the outcome to effective training but also identified additional improvements.

When we get unexpected outcomes, whether in our organization or in our personal lives, this is a template for what we should do. Don't assume you're that good. Assess, evaluate, search for patterns, and identify causational factors. This is a practice of exceptional professionals.

ESSAY 28

Marrying

There's no decision in your life that will be as consequential as who you marry. You're going to travel through life with this woman. If you have children, raising them will be in partnership with your wife. You'll collaborate with your wife as you navigate the questions of life, such as moving out of state for a job, what house to buy, how to furnish it, and where to go on vacation. When you encounter difficulties, your wife will support or aggravate the situation. Older couples know that "for better or worse" is not a cute phrase but rather a serious commitment. No other aspect of your life—not income, acclaim, or financial success—will impact the quality of your life as much as having a wife who's the right one for you.

A successful marriage requires constant attention. How could it be otherwise? Two people, unaware of their flaws, join together for everyday routine interactions and the big decisions. The more that you have in common, the better. This includes shared values, religious beliefs, finances, education, and aspirations. Sometimes, a man is drawn to his opposite—a woman who is outgoing and social to counter his quiet, contemplative personality. While you may be drawn to someone with different personality attributes, understand this is a recipe for conflict.

Why are you drawn to a woman as a potential wife? Is it because she needs you? Is it because you need her? Emotionally mature and healthy people don't marry unhealthy people. Ambitious people don't marry lazy ones. People who have, and work toward, long-term financial goals don't marry spendthrifts. Kind people don't marry mean ones. Conversely, immature or emotionally needy people marry others with emotional needs. Lonely people marry lonely people. This is codependency.

Are you attracted to her because she brings you joy? Do you want to make her life better? The answer to both questions needs to be yes. This is a lifelong partnership, and you need to be equally yoked. Pay particular attention to what your siblings and close friends think about this woman as a potential wife.

Where will you find this woman? To use military parlance, college is a *target-rich environment*. After college, the workplace is where many meet their spouses. This is because people drawn to the same field have much in common. If you work in a male-dominated field, finding a wife is going to require greater effort. A third avenue is friends. You spend time with people who are like you. Importantly, they know you. This is why, when asked how they met, so many people say a friend introduced them.

ESSAY 29

Mentors and Sages

One of the core attributes of men is our drive to be independent. Our heroes—whether historical, current, or fictional—are independent. The first painting I bought was that of a mountain man. I was in my early forties and still retained an aspiration of being self-sufficient. But strengths come with corresponding weaknesses. The downside of our proclivity to be self-reliant is that we're averse to ask for assistance. Women getting exasperated with men for not stopping to ask for directions is an example of this. Life is tough enough as it is without making it more difficult by refusing to ask more experienced men for their perspective.

A few men pursue mentors and sages. A mentor is someone experienced and successful in an endeavor that you want to pursue. We most commonly think of mentors in the workplace. In the pursuit of professional aspirations, we look at someone in our field who has mastered what we want to achieve. What are the ingredients for success? Most likely, this recipe is a combination of hard lessons learned, relationships, unwritten rules, clients and situations to avoid, reading recommendations, and personal disciplines. You pursue a mentor because *you* know what you want.

Successful mentor-protégé relationships are the exception. This is because, too often, the protégé presumes that he just needs to show up. The mentor is the more knowledgeable one who will ask the right questions and then guide the protégé. This doesn't work. The predominant responsibility lies with the protégé. What is it that he wants to learn or improve? Perhaps it's how to close a sale or how to allocate your time or how to choose the most valuable industry events. Identify what you consider to be your most pressing shortcoming and ask for counsel on this specific topic. During the course of conversations, your mentor will identify other improvement areas for you to pursue. This occurs naturally and is incidental. A mentor is *not* a psychologist, who has the responsibility to ask probing questions until he eventually determines the areas in which you need to improve.

When you ask someone to mentor you, ask for a finite time period. Perhaps one hour, once a month, for a year. If at the end of a year, you and the mentor want to continue the relationship, then you're free to do so. Always be on time for these meetings. If you waste the mentor's valuable time, he'll terminate the relationship, and you'll have harmed your reputation with someone influential in your field.

If you effectively use mentors, you'll have several over the years. You'll change directions and identify someone else who can help you with the next phase of your growth. This is another reason for a finite time commitment.

Sages differ from mentors. Sages are older insightful men who have experience across multiple disciplines and have a life perspective (as opposed to a professional one). You want to ask a sage for his time when you're at life-transition points, and you *don't* know what to do.

ESSAY 30

Near-Term Goals

If you're conscientious with your life, don't make any major mistakes, and don't encounter debilitating misfortune; the time will come when you'll be positioned to pursue contentment. But this comes later in life. Since these essays are directed toward young men, I'll address the narrower topic of near-term goals.

Well-meaning people tell young men to develop a life plan. Picture yourself at the age of sixty. What were your family relationships, career achievements, friendships, and finances? I consider this faulty counsel. When you're twenty-eight, it's all but impossible to see yourself at sixty. You're still exploring. You're still discovering what the workplace alternatives are. Do you have a good job and a bad boss? Are you in the wrong field? What kind of jobs and employers exist that might be an ideal fit? If you haven't yet found a wife, you're unlikely to have intimate experience with how other families function. Your interests in sports, civic engagement, and travel are still evolving. Not only do you not yet know what's out there, you don't yet know yourself well. Your life is dynamic. In your twenties, you should have a vision of where you'd like to be in five years. In your thirties, you should have better-defined goals of where you'd like to be in ten years. In your forties, you should be pursuing twenty-year aspirations.

There's a plethora of self-help books that assist at this stage of life. Some you can scan in an hour. In others, you'll find profound insights. You'll highlight paragraphs that describe yourself and/or your difficulties more precisely than you can. Blogs, podcasts, articles, and books are helpful tools, but be wary of thinking you've attained final clarity into who you are and where you fit in the world. When you read a headline like the "Five Keys to a Successful Life," don't believe it. There may be useful practices, but you're unique, and your aspirations, goals, understanding, and friendships should evolve.

I place the impediments to personal success into two categories: the small ones and the big ones. You will continue to have everyday annoyances. This could be an uncooperative coworker, canceled vacation flights, and rude people. Learn to accept these. Keep the irritants of life in perspective.

Then there are the really important matters. The opening line of *Anna Karenina* is "Happy families are all alike; every unhappy family is unhappy in its own way." Tolstoy's point is that contented families share the same characteristics of respectful spouses, loving parents who are aligned on child-rearing, a long-range perspective, and equanimity during the tough times. Conversely, each unhappy family is so because of particular flaws. It may be meanness, alcoholism, finances, in-laws, clinical depression, or something else. Tolstoy's insight applies to other aspects of our lives as well. You'll be unable to achieve personal success if one of the big issues present in your life is unresolved.

ESSAY 31

Perseverance

One of the most enduring values of American culture is that of perseverance. The Pilgrims persevered in a risky transatlantic voyage and established themselves in the harsh New England environment. The Oregon Trail pioneers persisted through untold hardships. According to Thomas Edison's notes, he failed 2,774 times before he achieved a working design of an electric light bulb. Colonel Sanders made 1,008 sales calls before a restaurant said yes to his Kentucky Fried Chicken recipe. Business magazines regularly carry stories of tenacity leading to eventual riches. This is who we are as Americans.

Our personal experiences also teach us how important it is to persist when we encounter challenges. On a hike, you'll never get to the mountaintop if you quit when you get tired. It's only through perseverance that you learned algebra. To succeed in athletics, you have to train harder than the other guy.

Conversely, being a *quitter* is a term of derision. As men, we are struck to the core when someone calls us a quitter.

However, for all its dividends, there are two important risks associated with tenacity. One is that it impedes experimentation. How will you know if you'll like an endeavor or interest if you don't give it a shot? Sometimes our fear of failure prevents us from even trying something new. All our lives, we should work at knowing ourselves better. Each time I discover something I'm not good it, it enables me to divert my energies to areas in which I'm likely to excel. How else can we discover our strengths and weaknesses if we don't experiment?

A second risk is our reluctance to quit when circumstances change. Job opportunities emerge and disappear. New information becomes available that alters our decisions. Technology changes. Business relationships change. Sometimes it becomes evident that the original decision was a mistake. A business tenet is "If you're going to fail, fail fast." This is so that you stop expending scarce resources on the wrong things. We need to adopt this practice in our personal lives.

This brings us to the crucial question: Am I quitting when I should persevere, or am I persevering when I should quit? Because of our egos, preferred beliefs, and emotional blind spots, it's difficult to determine the right answer. Be as objective as possible. Write a list of pros and cons. This is when it's especially valuable to have confidants and mentors. Ask them for their perspective.

ESSAY 32

Personality Types

The world is full of fascinating people. The type of a mind that is drawn to pursue architecture and design a hospital is much different than that of an actor. The reason we enjoy the standard of living that we have is because of virologists, soldiers, metallurgists, economists, teachers, administrators, artists, ship designers, traffic engineers, psychologists, logisticians, geneticists, and hundreds of more specialists. Why are people drawn to these fields?

In order to succeed in life, both personally and professionally, we need to understand, appreciate, and effectively work with people whose minds don't work like ours. Even the most casual observer notices that someone is kind, a constant critic, avoids conflict, or is detail-oriented. This is helpful in interacting with an individual. But to become more effective, we need a more systematic approach to understanding personality differences.

Fortunately, there's been ample research into personality types. One of the oldest is the *Meyers-Briggs Type Indicator*. There are several others including the *DiSC*, the *Color Personality Test*, and the *Judgment Index*. My personal preference is the *Big Five personality traits*. A typical reaction when taking one of these tests is delight. The assessment succinctly describes your personality. With our ego fully engaged, it's not uncommon to see the superiority of our way of thinking.

I was the founder of a company that performed analytical work. When the employees took a personality test, we discovered that we didn't have anyone who scored high on emotional engagement, empathy, and leniency. Of course not. Such a person would not have been drawn to a company doing analytical work.

Understanding personality types is a start. But it's the amateurs who stop when they feel like they've seen themselves in the mirror. The expert takes this understanding to the next level. Anticipate when conflict and low cooperation are likely. An example is a banker who works with a nonprofit. The visionary, compassionate nonprofit leader orients on client needs and will be frustrated by the constraints imposed by the banker. I've sat in multiple meetings where visionary leaders describe changes to be pursued, and the engineers in the room delve deeper and deeper into the details of the plan. The big-picture leader and the detail-oriented engineers are frustrated by the discussion.

It's inevitable, even helpful, to have differing perspectives. I've seen potentially consequential mistakes avoided because someone with specialized knowledge introduced a consideration that was contrary to the direction the conversation was going.

My counsel is threefold: Be cautious in accepting positions where the boss sees the world differently than you do. Don't expect everyone to have your perspective; rather anticipate that they'll see the situation differently. Third, communicate in their language rather than yours. Discuss the topic by addressing the considerations that are important to them.

ESSAY 33

Problems

Throughout life, we encounter problems. Some are small and some are consequential. We have professional and personal problems. As a general statement, American men have a bias for action. Too often, we jump into resolving a problem before we've taken the time to identify what kind of a problem we have and what the alternatives are. There's validity to the fortune cookie saying, "*A problem clearly stated is a problem half solved.*" Determine what type of a problem you have. Then before jumping into action, pause, and write a problem statement. (Crises are an exception to this practice.)

Crises are narrow in definition, have a short-term duration, and require immediate attention. Typically, we have to stop what we're doing and turn our attention to an unexpected immediate problem. I came home from work one day to find fire trucks in the driveway. Our house had extensive smoke damage and was uninhabitable. The immediate problems included where we were going to spend the night and what we were going to wear tomorrow. Whatever your plans were, they're immediately altered.

Narrowly defined problems typically have only one or two causes. Your employer is closing the office where you work. Your choices are to move to Chicago or take a small severance payment and find another job. These problems need a remedy, but not in the next hour.

Sometimes it's difficult to identify the true problem. Perhaps you're frustrated at work. You can't figure out why. You have a good boss. Your compensation is good. You like your coworkers. Why are you disgruntled? It takes a few weeks of contemplation until you come to the insight that you just aren't suited to this type of work. Oftentimes, just acknowledging the problem relieves stress. The next question is what to do. In personal situations, we typically face three choices: accept it, change it, or leave it.

Systemic problems occur in organizations. This is a problem, not of an individual but of *the system*. We get frustrated when we repeatedly encounter similar problems. This is because we've misdiagnosed the problem as a narrowly defined one when, in fact, it's a systemic issue. As an example, you work for a nonprofit, and you're repeatedly frustrated because they don't engage in goal setting and accountability. The problem isn't your boss or that relevant performance data isn't being collected. This is an organization filled with compassionate people who focus on fundraising and caring for the needy. It's unlikely that accountability and efficiency are ever going to be important. This is the nature of the beast.

Later in life, if you become a senior leader, you'll have to address *transformative problems* and *complex problems with unknown unknowns*. Finally, in our society, we have *wicked problems* (although I prefer the term *mess*). These are issues that can only be mitigated, not solved. Examples are crime, homelessness, illegal immigration, and addictions.

ESSAY 34

Reading

There are several ways we learn. We begin by asking questions. Between the ages of two and five, a child asks an average of forty thousand questions. Unfortunately, by the time we're adults, many unlearn this practice. There are exceptions. As commander of the Grande Armée, Napoleon Bonaparte stunned lieutenants by asking questions they considered so basic. I'm confident you know men who constantly ask questions. How do things work? Why is the process done this way? What is your story? Why do you have this perspective on this position?

From childhood, we learn in classrooms with prepared curricula and professional teachers.

Of course, we learn by doing. Sometimes this is applying the principles learned in a classroom. Preparing your own tax returns is instructive. Perhaps you watch a YouTube video to replace a toilet.

We learn by watching others. We learn from listening to their stories and reading about the successes and failures of others. Learning from others is far less expensive than learning from our own mistakes.

We learn by reading. Until the invention of television, Americans spent hours each day reading. Admirable leaders were avid readers. But today, half of American men didn't read a book last year. This is tragic self-sabotage. Consider a man who, from age twenty to sixty, reads 1 book a year. Over this time span, he will have read 40 books. His neighbor, who read a book a month, will have read 480. I know men who read 30–40 books a year. Over forty years, that's 1,500 books.

It's not that readers don't also learn by conversations, questioning, doing, and watching others. They have the *additional* advantage of reading. Also, books have the advantage of giving you information and insight that is outside your normal profession and experiences.

Resolve to read a book a month. This doesn't even require time diverted from watching sports, TikTok videos, or playing video games. Every time you know you're going to wait, have a book that you're reading. This is doctor's appointments, your daughter's swim practice, airports, and airplanes. Simply using wait time gets you to a book a month.

You should read books that provide greater knowledge in your professional field. Read good fiction to learn how to better express yourself. Read history to learn about humanity and better predict how people are going to react and events are going to unfold.

Consider the growth, the advantage you'll have, a decade from now when you've read 120 more books than your coworker. A curious, growing man constantly wants to get better in every aspect of his life. To forgo books is indifference or negligence. You're better than that.

ESSAY 35

Reliability

When we write a résumé, we list our academic credentials, work experience, recognitions, and achievements. This is necessary to get past the first gate and be invited to an interview. During the interview, candidates endeavor to impress a prospective hiring manager with their creativity, technically savvy, cleverness, enthusiasm, and their team-collaboration abilities. For the most part, all of this is necessary.

Put yourself in your boss's shoes. He/she has deadlines, performance goals, and needs to provide clear directions and guide subordinates. He/she also spends a considerable amount of attention addressing the things that aren't going well. This includes changes from above, prickly clients, scarce resources, and difficult employees. If you want to get assigned to certain projects and be considered for promotion, you need to focus on making your boss look good and lessening his/her workload.

Managers have the unenviable job of being responsible for goals being met and, at the same time, not micromanaging. The most valued and underrated attribute you can bring is reliability. Show up on time. Every day. Perform your work in a timely manner that requires minimal oversight or correction by your boss. Simply going to work every day and diligently doing what you're supposed to puts you in the top fifth of your peers. When you encounter an unexpected obstacle or need guidance, promptly inform your boss. If I were the hiring manager interviewing, I might ask the question "Why should I hire you?" Then the candidate responds, "I'll do what I said I'd do and do it on time. You'll never have to check up on me." Very likely, I'd ask for a short recess, call his references to confirm the truth of his claim, and then immediately offer him the position.

Within six months, you want your supervisor to know that he/she doesn't need to check on the timeliness or quality of your work. When layoffs come, you want your boss to immediately identify you as one to be retained. When important projects come along that have the potential to accelerate your career, you want to be considered because you're reliable.

In my junior high school band, I played the trombone. We were a marching band, so everyone had to memorize the music. One day, our obviously irritated band leader entered the band room. He called on individual students to play a piece. Seven or eight students did. The rest of us were looking at our shoes praying that he didn't call on us. I vowed never again to be one who was being pulled along by those more conscientious. What I learned that day was that there were a few students who carried the rest of us. I've seen this pattern repeated in every organization I've seen.

Be reliable. Be tenacious. Be the one who everyone recognizes as one of the few who are head and shoulders above your peers. Unseen by you, every day, your reputation is being established.

ESSAY 36

Sages

For some reason, *sage* is not part of everyday vocabulary. Is this because we prefer being inundated with knowledge rather than wisdom? Is it because a foundational element of wisdom is truth, and we no longer believe in truth?

Sages exist in our society. They're rare (and always will be), but they're around. When I ask men what sages they know, the typical response is someone famous, someone they don't know. When pressed to identify someone they personally know, it's evident from the ensuing pause that men haven't given thought to this.

The sages I know are over seventy. I suspect this is because they need to have completed the major life transitions. Examples include the difficult transitions from full-time work to a fulfilling retirement life and the successful shift to an adult-to-adult relationship with children. They're financially secure (which is *not* the same as wealthy). They know themselves. They neither err by being too arrogant nor too humble. This also means they don't accept invitations to contribute in areas they lack expertise. They're more interested in listening than telling. When their counsel is sought, they ask increasingly probing questions to guide the seeker to discover his own solution.

Surprisingly, sages have common backgrounds. They've had experience across disciplines. They've overcome significant professional and/or personal failures. They constantly ask questions. They are well-traveled and have read more than one thousand books. This is consistent with their unrelenting curiosity. They've lived a full and varied life and reflect deeply on these experiences and those of others.

If you're in your thirties, you may not know a sage. If this is the case, ask someone in his fifties. Ask to be introduced. At least five times a year, invite the sage to go out for a meal with you (you buy). Don't ask him for quick-and-easy answers. Rather tell him about yourself and the decisions you face. Ask him to hold up a mirror to help you see yourself more accurately. Ask what you're missing when you frame questions and options. When the time comes for major life decisions, you'll be immensely grateful that you've established a relationship with a sage.

If you don't have a sage in your life, I ask, why not? Think of a historical sage or a current one whom you know by his fame. If it were possible to have a two-hour conversation with him, you'd pay a high price for the opportunity, but there are quiet sages in your community who are not well-known. In fact, although they are men of exceptional insight, they often avoid fame. Why would you not avail yourself of such a resource?

ESSAY 37

Semantics

Words have meaning. This may appear to be a trite statement, but it isn't. As an example, in the pursuit of a goal, how do you respond when someone calls you *driven* or when they use the term *inflexible*? In this context, the two words are practically synonymous. But the connotations are entirely different.

Skilled sales people carefully choose terms to influence your thinking. On the sales floor of the car dealership, the salesman will tell you what a great *investment* this truck will be. An *investment* is something you purchase because either you expect to sell it later at a higher price, or you anticipate income from it. The purchase of a car is an *expenditure*. You're going to use the truck for a few years and then trade it in or sell it for an amount less than you paid for it. We're much more drawn to the notion of investing in something than we are incurring an expense.

But the task is greater than to avoid being tricked by others. If we're not careful with words, we fool ourselves. A young wife gets pregnant, and the couple says, "We *need* to buy a house." But this isn't true. Infants have been, and continue to be, successfully raised in apartments. The truth is the couple *wants* to buy a house. A *need* is compelling. A *want* is optional. This is not an argument against buying a house. Rather it's an argument for clear thinking.

The use of particular terms has a subtle yet insidious effect on our thinking. We incur debt because we tell ourselves that we *need* new furniture, a nice restaurant dinner, sports equipment, a Caribbean vacation, three streaming services, and a new vehicle. One is compelled to respond to a need. Agency and responsibility are removed.

The misuse of words is not restricted to faulty financial decisions. We misuse terminology to avoid hard truths with our health, time, friendships, church, pursuit of goals, and serving others. We want to avoid self-inflicted deceit. A good place to start is precision in the words we use.

ESSAY 38

Stories

For 10,000 years, humans have been telling stories. While sitting around the fire, boys and young men listened to the stories of the elders. When travelers came to spend the night in the village, people were eager to hear their stories about different places, people, and customs. The *Travels of Marco Polo* was published and distributed 150 years before the invention of the printing press.

Stories are the richest form of communications. I can recite stories my mother told from her childhood, from a different era than ours. Yesterday, at lunch, a friend told a story about how the United States Military Academy taught cadets to become gentlemen, specifically, gave them dance instruction. Why are stories so impactful? We learn about a different time and situation. We learn about the naivete or wisdom of the storyteller. A good story includes tragedy, humor, fortune, suspense, and insights we can apply to our lives.

Professionals know the value of stories. Law school students are instructed to present the jury with a compelling story. Advertisers are masters at brief stories. When it came time to create a name for my company, I created a word that emanated from a practice in early American history. People would ask me the origin of the company name. After I told them the story, they never forgot it.

We've moved away from listening to stories. This is an unfortunate societal change. There's a sense that what's important are piecemeal facts. Conduct a quick Internet search to learn the essential facts. But this brings narrow knowledge. To gain wisdom, you need to know what to ask. You need context. You need understanding. You need to be able to contrast this situation to a similar one. There's no better means to achieve this than to listen to stories.

Ask your grandparents about their stories. Ask your parents. When you encounter people with different experiences, ask them about their story. Ask successful people in your career field about their stories.

A common mistake is to not understand that the setting is paramount. Five minutes before your extended family is sitting down for dinner is not the time or setting to ask your grandfather to tell you about the most difficult year of his life. You need to dedicate your full attention for twenty to thirty minutes to hear this story. It needs to be in an environment without interruptions. If you're on a driving trip or in a setting of extended one-on-one time, set down your phone and ask for stories. In your profession, ask someone you admire if you can take them to lunch because you want to hear their story of the difficulties he/she encountered in his/her career progression.

Finally, carefully watch and learn from raconteurs. Become one. People are drawn to good storytellers.

ESSAY 39

Stress

When we have high work demands, strained relationships, and/or limited choices, we say we're stressed. Emotional stress drains us. It saps our joy. Persistent stress adversely affects our physical health as well as our mental well-being. Also, we deceive ourselves when we don't acknowledge the adverse effect prolonged stress has on those around us. Your wife, your children, and your friendships suffer the effects.

But I suggest we err by only thinking of stress in negative terms. Consider a life without stress. What would that look like? Perhaps a job that is below your capabilities. Every day is easy. There are no challenges. There's no growth. There are no personal achievements. You aren't contributing, and you're not becoming more capable. In most instances, you'd start looking for a new position. One that includes challenges and learning; that is, one with stress.

You should want stress in your life. You should pursue difficult assignments, undertakings that are a stretch but not too much of one. When you're a presenter, you want to be a bit nervous. Otherwise you'll come across as boring. Challenges, a.k.a. *stress*, are the source of personal growth and the satisfaction that comes from doing something well that few others can do.

The obvious challenge is how to craft your life with the right amount of stress. I have a brother who is a receiver. When there's fraud, the court appoints him as a receiver to locate and preserve assets to eventually be sold with the funds distributed to defrauded investors and creditors. When he accepts cases, he knows that the first few weeks will be frantic. Then the workload largely settles down to a manageable pace. But because he may have four cases at any given time, there will be times when court cases, lawsuits, auctions, and depositions coincide. He accepts that he'll have stressful periods (due to high workload). This is part of the job. The key is these spikes are of short duration.

Look at the work stress in your life. If there's too little, it's likely that you'll want to find another position. If there are periods of high stress, but they aren't of long of duration, accept that this is a reason you're in your role. If your workload stress is extended, you need to change something. Not only for yourself but for those around you.

We rarely succeed in getting this right each week. This is because in both our professional and personal lives, we get hit with unexpected surprises. Regardless of the causes, if the stressful periods in your life come and go, accept this as life. If the duration extends for long periods, change something.

ESSAY 40

The Future

I know a few men who have led predictable lives. I have a son-in-law who, when he was twelve years old, wrote a letter to United Airlines informing them that he wanted to be an airline pilot. United Airlines responded with a polite form letter that listed the eligibility requirements to become one of their pilots. When he was twenty-eight, interviewing for a pilot opening, he handed to the panel the sixteen-year-old form letter and said, "I did it." Today he's a United Airlines pilot flying transatlantic routes.

But for the majority of us, our lives unfold with twists and turns we couldn't have envisioned. Assume that someone asked me to look ahead ten years and predict what my life would be like in foundational areas like my employer, home address, regular friends, financial assets, and near-term goals. At no point in my life would I have been 50 percent accurate.

One of the reasons we are such poor predictors of the future is we change. John Eldridge identifies six stages of the full masculine journey of life; that of *boy, cowboy, warrior, lover, king,* and *sage.* Reflect on the person you were ten years ago. What were your interests, concerns, and aspirations? If there's a distinct contrast to where you are today, you're normal. And this will likely be the case a decade from now.

We underestimate how much we'll change. We also tend to think the world is more constant than it is. Technology developments alter jobs and affect our personal lives. Cultural values change. Laws and taxes change. Hopefully, we become more knowledgeable. If we're intentional, we become more insightful. Opportunities emerge that we didn't see coming. We encounter setbacks and diversions that couldn't be anticipated. We have ideas as to what our careers will be like, our marriages, home, wealth, and children. These are illusions. We can't know such things.

When the unexpected comes, don't get frustrated. This is a sign of naivete, that you know and control more than you do. You're not always going to relish unexpected and (sometimes) undesired changes. But you'll experience less stress in your life if you understand this is inevitable.

ESSAY 41

The Halo Effect

One of the delusions we succumb to is the *halo effect*. We want an orderly world. We want to believe that there are stellar people who have figured everything out and excel in all aspects of life. Autobiographies, magazines, TED Talk presenters, newscasts, and social media all feed this illusion. Listen to speaker introductions. The purpose of the introduction is to give the speaker credibility, to tell you why you made the right decision to be in this audience. You're about to hear valuable knowledge from this highly accomplished esteemed speaker. We're not disappointed. The presenter knows much more than we do about the topic, be it city planning, immunology, demographics, the Pompeii ruins, or geopolitics.

In some fields, professionals are overt in letting you know they have greater expertise than you do. Physicians wear white lab coats, professors use the title doctor, judges wear black robes, and the uniforms of military officers display their rank. But we err when we succumb to the halo effect. We're rightfully impressed with someone because he/she has expertise, achievements, and esteem in his/her niche. Too often, we make the implicit, often unrecognized, assumption that the person is better than we are. I know accomplished scientists who aren't a friend to anyone, generals who are poor husbands, unethical professors, successful business executives who are lousy fathers, financially inept physicians, and mean-spirited architects.

Shortly after I sold my company, due to unexpected circumstances, I became the head of a private K–12 Christian school. Because this position was well outside my areas of expertise, it was only with great reluctance (and desperation on the part of the school board) that I accepted the role. What I soon learned was that educators considered successful businessmen to be more accomplished than themselves. Consequently, I entered the role with more credibility than I deserved. (No, I didn't dissuade them of their notions. I needed all the credibility I could muster.)

In the professional arena, respect and learn from accomplished people. They have greater knowledge than you do in their particular field. But remember, this expertise is in a narrow slice of life. Don't take financial advice from an astrophysicist. Be selectively deferential.

With respect to your personal life, decide your important values. I know several men whom I admire for their accomplishments. But I wouldn't invite them to my home for dinner.

ESSAY 42

The Ideal Day

Consider what an ideal day would entail. Depending on your interests, it might be sailing, hunting, bicycling with friends, gambling at a Las Vegas casino, spending an afternoon at the pool, or attending an evening rock concert. Whatever your ideal day is, it's likely a day of leisure. A day free of obligations. We can extend this exercise and contemplate an ideal week. Whether it's due to an aggravating day at work, or we're planning a vacation, we often think about this topic. We become worn down by obligations, decisions, and stressful circumstances. We long to have the opportunity to spend time doing what brings us pleasure.

Next, consider what the next decade will be like if all your aspirations came to fruition. We know how empty a life is without work. People win the lottery. I know a man who became a dot-com millionaire when he was young. After a few months, these men are miserable. They don't have friends (because their former friends are at work!). They don't have any challenges. They aren't growing. No one needs them. They aren't contributing. They have no purpose. One can only play so long.

Men confuse an ideal day with an ideal life. A satisfying life includes stressful days when you prevail. It includes doing something well that others can't do. It includes new challenges that bring growth. It includes love and friends. It includes meeting commitments.

It includes doing something for others. It includes being needed. Margaret Thatcher said, "Look at a day when you are supremely satisfied at the end. It's not a day when you lounged around doing nothing. It's a day you've had everything to do, and you've done it."

Contrast this with a vacation. The literal definition of vacation is to *vacate* from your normal activities. The word means freedom from something. Having complete freedom from everything would be great for a week. But it would be a miserable life.

Reread Rudyard Kipling's poem "How to Be a Man." One gains discernment, patience, perspective, and insight by being in the arena. Your work, friends, and contributions add much more to your life than the breaks from it.

ESSAY 43

The Next Decade

On a British Isles cruise, I met a delightful young actress who was a member of the entertainment troupe. She was more skilled than the others, and at one point, I asked her about her aspirations. Where would she like to be in five years? Because I spend so much time with conscientious people, I expected she'd say something about London's West End. But she gaily responded, "Oh, I don't like to think about things like that." Perhaps good fortune will strike, she'll be *discovered* by someone in the industry, and she'll advance in her career. But I'd bet against that outcome. I know of no one who reached his/her career aspirations who didn't doggedly pursue a goal.

I know young people who say, "I'm going to go back to college one day." With such wispy statements, they most assuredly won't. When I meet young men in their twenties, I'll often ask, "Where do you want to be in five years?" For men in their thirties, I'll more often ask about the next decade. Their responses are telling. Some young men haven't thought about this. Some intentionally (albeit, perhaps, unconsciously) don't think about this because to do so would be to recognize that they are drifting along to wherever the stream takes them.

Successful men have goals and corresponding action plans. Explicit goals may be to establish relationships with a given number of professionals in their fields, to engage in a mentor-protégé relationship, and/or attain certifications. Their professional goal may be "I plan to be a branch manager," or "I'm going to open my own veterinary practice," or "I'll become an invited presenter at my industry conferences." Their personal goals may be more travel, becoming more fit, deepening friendships, or becoming a kinder person. Without exception, the men I know who have or are on track to meet their goals have action plans. When I ask, "What have you done in the past three months to progress toward this goal?" they have an immediate answer.

Progressing toward goals is often accompanied by unexpected twists and turns. You get a surprise job offer from another company that moves you ahead faster than you expected. You get an inept boss who impedes your progress. Also, as you learn more about opportunities and yourself, you may change your goal. But you're constantly asking yourself what you've done over the past few months to progress closer to your goal.

ESSAY 44

The Path Not Taken

For some reason, we look back at decisions made and wonder whether they were the right ones. What if I had attended the other university? What if I had been bold enough to ask that girl out for a date? What if I had selected that field of study? What would my life have been like if I had accepted that job offer? When we engage in this hindsight thinking, we invariably develop notions that life would have been better if we'd made the other choice. But this is erroneous and harmful thinking. It's impossible to know where that path would have taken us.

A month after joining the Army, when I was in basic training, a few of us were called out to attend a presentation. Someone had reviewed all of our records and identified those of us who were single, under twenty-one years old, and had attained a high score on the Army's intelligence test. Three officers told us that we were eligible to attend a yearlong preparatory school and then the United States Military Academy. I'd probably heard of West Point, but I didn't know what it was. The officers assumed that we all knew this was an invitation to attend one of the most prestigious Ivy League universities in the country. I didn't know that and declined to apply. I glance back at that juncture and ask myself how my life would have been different had I made a different decision that day.

Perhaps I would have become a stellar military officer. Or maybe I would have met the minimum time in service, and armed with a degree from such a highly esteemed university, I could have excelled in the corporate world. But such wishful thinking is faulty to the core. Maybe I would have withdrawn within a few weeks because I wasn't willing to tolerate the grueling *Beast Barracks* environment. It may have been that I wasn't proficient enough in math or English to succeed. The fact is, I have no idea where that path would have taken me.

Avoid succumbing to this trap of hindsight wishful thinking. When we do this, we envision that our lives would have been better. We never think that the outcome might have been worse. Such speculation results in remorse. Don't think this way. We have ample real challenges in which we need to prevail. It's folly to add imaginary regrets.

ESSAY 45

The Thinking of Others

One of the most repeated, erroneous, and consequential mistakes we make is thinking we know the motives of others. We see someone standing in the center of the walkway texting, and we think, *How can you be so self-absorbed and inconsiderate that you don't stand to the side and let others pass by?* This judgment may be accurate. Or it could well be that the person is just oblivious. There are people who are inattentive to their surroundings. We sense the irritation of a boss or coworker when we ask a question or want to coordinate an action. But it may well be that the person is focused on writing a document or solving a problem. If you said, "When you're free, I'd like to talk to you about something," you may get a helpful, even enjoyable, conversation fifteen minutes later. A husband agrees to help with housework. Then his wife gets exasperated with him because he doesn't see the obvious need for vacuuming. But he really doesn't see such things. If she said, "Sometime today, will you vacuum the living room?" she might be surprised by his willing reply.

Some people are quick thinkers. Radio talk show hosts and comedians immediately reply to comments. For others, the ideal response comes to them later. On a business trip, on the way from the airport to my hotel, I stopped at a grocery store for a small purchase. The store was in a poorer area of the city. At the checkout line, the fellow in front of me didn't have enough cash for the ten-pound bag of potatoes he intended to purchase. The cashier shrugged, took the bag of potatoes, and the man slumped off. Five minutes later, I chastised myself. "Why didn't you hand the requisite change to the cashier so the man could have bought the potatoes?"

Some people are more observant than others. Some people immediately see how they can assist, while others don't see the opportunity to assist until it's pointed out to them. I once had an employee tell me that the reason I didn't give the promotion to her is because I didn't like her. I was prejudiced toward overweight people.

I said, "That's amazing. How does this ability work out for you?"

She replied, "What ability?"

I said, "This ability to see what's in the hearts of others."

There are times when we've seen such consistent behavior that we're confident that we can assess the other person. I know people who are genuinely selfish. But more often, we don't know the other person's motives. Does he behave this way because he's insecure, or is he truly that arrogant? I've had employees say, "I thought you were mad when I gave you that news." I apologize and tell them that I err by digesting information and not thinking to reply. My silence is incorrectly interpreted as annoyance.

We're either naive or arrogant when we suppose that other people see things the way we do, or they think like we do. Before attributing motives, pause and ask the person their rationale or if you're accurate in your impressions. The vast majority of the time, this practice reduces conflict and contributes to constructive communications.

ESSAY 46

Time Management

I've counseled scores of entrepreneurs. One of my recurring observations is that the business owner doesn't have enough time. He or she is doing everything possible to hold the company together, hire and retain the right employees, pursue new customers, ensure high quality, minimize costs through operational excellence, develop and pursue strategic plans, and manage myriad other responsibilities. I tell these business owners that there is no resource more constrained than the senior leader's time. You can buy more equipment, lease more space, borrow more money, and better utilize available software. But the one resource you cannot increase is your time and attention.

This same principle applies to our personal lives. A week consists of 168 hours. This applies to every one of us. Subtract the time required to sleep, eat, shower, commute, and other basic functions, and we each have around 100 hours a week.

Hardly a day goes by without me hearing someone say, "I'm so busy!" I presume people say this to convey how much they're doing. It's a badge of honor. But what I hear is either they don't establish priorities or are unable to adhere to them. Once, I was being briefed by a team engaged in a two-year-project. Twenty minutes into the presentation, I interrupted to say, "I'm only slightly interested in your activities. What I want to know is your progress." This goal-oriented mindset also applies to our personal lives. Being busy is of no value. Progress toward what really matters is what high achievers do.

Deliberate and then write a time budget to identify how you'll ideally use next week's one hundred hours. How many hours will you spend working? How many hours meeting with friends? If you're married, how many hours with your wife and/or children? How many hours for physical fitness, your hobby, reading, playing video games, or watching movies? How many restorative hours will you spend on yourself? Next, beginning Sunday morning, record how you spent your time. Break it down into fifteen-minute segments. Don't ignore something as an exception. Rather be disciplined with this exercise. At the end of the week, compare your ideal time allocation with how you spent the one hundred hours.

More than any other practice, this is the recipe for success. We deceive ourselves when we say we don't have time to get to something. Others have learned how to read more, nurture relationships, serve others, care for themselves, go to the art museum, and have the energy to work on what's important. If you don't carefully manage your time, it's because you're lazy or don't want to. Consider your peer who spends ten more hours a week reading technical journals, writing thank-you notes, or learning about developments in related fields. In a decade, he'll have invested 5,200 more hours in his career. You'll never catch up.

This isn't to suggest that you shouldn't have leisure. On the contrary, you should. My counsel is to be intentional about that leisure, restorative time.

ESSAY 47

Tribes

We're predisposed to spend time with familiar people. Add to this our preference to associate with people of similar interests, and the result is people in the same field predominantly spending time with each other. Physicians have common interests. They attend professional seminars, and those in the local area know each other on a first-name basis. They even separate themselves into subgroups. At local-association meetings, during the social time, you'll see the surgeons in one corner and the radiologists gathered somewhere else. In all sorts of career fields, you'll see the same phenomena. Firemen, Realtors, architects, restaurateurs, and engineers spend time with each other.

In your twenties, you should attend professional-association seminars and social gatherings. These are the settings in which you learn from the best in your field. It's also where you'll get noticed. But a common error is only spending time in this tribe. When this happens, you become increasingly narrow in your view of the world. In taking the easy path, you limit your horizons and understanding.

Take the initiative to associate with professionals from outside your field. An effective means is to join a civic organization. An example is a Rotary or Rotaract Club. When I participated in our community's *leadership* program (https://alpleaders.org), I met a hospital CEO, the director of the botanical garden, investment bankers, and others whom I never would have encountered had I not expanded my circle. I learned from each one of these leaders, and some became friends.

A few years ago, while driving cross-country, four of us stopped for dinner at a Mexican restaurant in Nebraska City. Seated at the adjacent table were ten to twelve men who were obvious friends. It was evident from their attire that they worked in different fields. As I listened, I recognized that they were members of the local Knights of Columbus fraternal organization. I was struck by how close-knit these men were. They were friends who learned from each other. I can't imagine that any of them thought their line of work was superior to that of another.

Find a way to work with and/or socially engage with people outside your field. The primary reasons you want to do this is to expand your horizons and to mitigate the risk that you become narrow minded. A secondary benefit is that you'll learn of practices that can be applied to your field. This is a distinctive advantage that you'll have over your peers who take the easy path and don't explore beyond the tribe.

ESSAY 48

Victimization

There are times in our lives when we get bad breaks. Another candidate got the job or promotion when we were more qualified. Because we're quiet and don't interrupt others in meetings, it's assumed that we don't have good ideas to contribute. A woman is attracted to a rough man she can tame rather than a man of character. You accept a position with another company, and the job is much different than you were led to believe. Someone who has the boss's ear makes denigrating remarks about you in order to remove your influence. You had flu the day a major proposal was scheduled, and whoever got tapped to give the presentation got credit for all your work. The examples are endless.

I'm not going to advise you to ignore this when it happens. You may well be justified in getting upset. But your response needs to be managed, both for professional and personal reasons.

When the injustice occurs in the workplace, you face a decision. If it's a small matter, it's often best to overlook it. It's important to not appear overly sensitive or emotional. If the harm is repetitive or significant, it may be best to raise this with your boss (after your emotions have subsided!). This largely depends on the personality of your supervisor. It's important that you don't communicate that your emotions should take precedence over the company needs. Strong emotions in the workplace are rarely helpful. On the contrary, they often result in irreparable harm to your status.

Among your close friends or with your wife, it's okay to vent your grievance. (Tell them upfront that you're just griping.) My experience is it's better to vent your frustrations than to deny them. Go have a beer with your friend and tell him you're angry with the injustice. If you have a wife, tell her. Complain. Grumble. Then get over it. I try to limit my lamenting to the remainder of the day. Occasionally, I've taken twenty-four hours to put the matter behind me, and a few times, it's taken a few days. If you allow yourself to think about the misdeed any longer, you risk bitterness, which is harmful in itself but also adversely affects future interactions and decisions. Secondly, a lengthy focus on the wrong impairs your ability to draw lessons from the experience.

Last week, I was in a conversation with a friend, and I asked him about being fired from an executive position. He described the power struggle and nepotism that led to this outcome. There was no resentment in his voice. Rather his body language and tone conveyed an understanding that this is the sort of thing that happens. His equanimity was one of the reasons he's a close friend.

Ask someone about undeserved bad breaks that came their way. Their attitude reveals much about their character. Even when you were the victim, you don't ever want to develop a victimization attitude.

ESSAY 49

Wealthy People

If you're fortunate, you'll have opportunities for social interactions with wealthy people. An example is a friend invites you to join him at his parents' beach house for the weekend. You arrive, and it's immediately obvious that these are really wealthy people. The father is friendly, and his wife is gracious. The couple seem to express a sincere interest in you. But you're intimidated by their wealth. They live a different life than you ever imagine you will. The cars they drive, the vacations they take, the restaurants they frequent, and the furnishings in their home are all reminders that they're successful, and you aren't.

In these encounters, don't withdraw. These are excellent opportunities to expand your understanding. I equate these occasions to when I encounter someone who grew up in a poor Brazilian village and now owns a successful local restaurant. There has to be a fascinating story here. Tell me about your journey.

When I first heard the terms *old money* and *new money*, I was astounded. You're rich! Isn't that good enough? Rich people differentiate themselves by how long their families have been wealthy? I've come to understand that, as a generalization, there's validity to these distinctions. *Old money* families consider their financial situation to be normal. In contrast, those who have been poor and, through luck and skill, have become financially secure are grateful to no longer worry about money.

People who have succeeded in becoming wealthy find that they have a decreasing circle of friends. They get few invitations to a neighborhood block party or to join the guys for a beer after work. Many are intimidated by their wealth and simply can't afford the join them in leisure activities.

Some wealthy people talk about taking their private airplane to spend a week in Roatan. Others talk about regrets over having to work such long hours when their children were teenagers. These conversations provide insight into whether they've become accustomed to their wealth or whether they remember (and likely enjoy) simple pleasures.

When you encounter wealthy people who want to spend time with you, embrace the opportunity. Perhaps this is someone successful in your career field who is willing to mentor you. Keep in mind the principle that relationships entail reciprocal courtesies. Don't make the mistake of assuming, because they have so much more money than you do, that they should always buy lunch. When it's your turn to buy, it's okay to take them to an affordable restaurant or even the burrito bus. It's important that they don't get the sense that you spend time with them in order to enjoy the luxuries they can provide.

ESSAY 50

Women

Because I'm old, I've spent a lot of time with women in personal and professional relationships. Given the centrality of women in our lives and my extensive experience with them, I'd like to write an essay about them. The problem is, I don't know enough to even write a paragraph, let alone a page. In fact, I all I know about women is they're not like us.

Have you ever met a male dental hygienist or kindergarten teacher? Yeah, me neither. As a general statement, men like things, and women like people. This is why construction equipment operators are men, and speech-language pathologists are predominantly women.

How many fifty-year-old women do you know who bought that car they dreamed of when they were teenagers but couldn't afford? They trailered it home, over the next two years, completely restored it, and now take it to car shows. The very notion is laughable. I've been in innumerable offices, ranging from machine tool sales to the Pentagon. Without exception, the office manager is a woman.

They share their hearts more than we do. They're more compassionate than we are. A recent medical study found the outcomes for male and female surgeons to be the same. But patients prefer female surgeons. Why? Because they're better listeners.

GRANDSON CONVERSATIONS

The differences start early. Two second-grade girls are walking and holding hands, while two boys are wrestling. Ask any middle-school teacher about their experiences. Women are different creatures from us.

The differences are evident by casual observations. Consider how the conversations change if there are only men present or if the group is coed. When couples meet socially, you see the men in one room talking about different topics than the women in the other room. This is all voluntary and natural.

We have a neighbor who has been a widow for a long time. She commented that she just wanted to sit down and have a conversation with a man. She said they think about different things.

Myriad studies consistently show that children fare better when raised in a home with a father and a mother. We do a poor job when we have to cover for the other sex. I know of a widowed mother who, every Saturday, dropped her nine-year-old boy off at the town barbershop for a few hours. She knew he needed to be around men.

I wince when I see men get exasperated with women because they don't think like us or communicate like us. They're not like us! Thanks be to God for this.

ABOUT THE AUTHOR

Ron Klein is a septuagenarian, one of the millions of baby boomers. He had a difficult, even cruel, father and left home when he was sixteen years old. He was captured, spent the night in a county juvenile detention center cell, and then placed in foster homes. He attended three different high schools but graduated, albeit in the middle of his class.

Nine months after graduating from high school, he enlisted in the Army. After the completion of jump (parachute) school, he went to Viet Nam, where he served as an infantryman conducting long-range reconnaissance patrols. Using the GI Bill, he got a baccalaureate degree in business (*cum laude*) and then a master's degree in economics (*magna cum laude*). He went back into the Army, this time as a commissioned officer, where he served as an armor officer, aviator, and in aircraft project management assignments.

His second career was that of an entrepreneur. In 1998, he founded Belzon, an aerospace services company. In 2003, *Inc.* magazine identified Belzon as the 202nd fastest-growing company in the country. After the company grew to one hundred employees, he sold it.

His third career was head of a Christian school. This was a turnaround position. The school was in dire circumstances and close to insolvency. Ten years later, the school achieved a status denoting it as one of the top 2 percent of Christian schools nationwide.

Ron has traveled to all fifty states and thirty-six countries. He holds an FAA commercial pilot's license with ratings in single and multiengine airplanes, seaplanes, and helicopters. Twelve times he led business-consulting teams to Da Nang, Viet Nam, to teach best business practices.

He's been an adjunct professor of economics at four universities. He's also been a high school debate coach and taught high school geopolitics classes. Twice, he took high school students to Vietnam. He also developed and taught a course on global technology and economic historical developments from AD 1500 and another one on the change in American households between 1860 and 1960.

He's served several civic roles in his community, including president of the Madison Rotary Club and chairman of the Huntsville Committee of 100. He's the founder of the community *Management Academy*, a nine-month program designed to teach best business practices to midlevel managers. He formed two *Veritas Forum* groups of men who meet monthly to discuss ideas.

He's read an estimated two thousand books and written four.

He and his wife, Sandra, live in Madison, Alabama.

Printed in the USA
CPSIA information can be obtained
at www.ICGtesting.com
LVHW041517081124
796065LV00002B/364